SHORT-TERM PLAY THERAPY FOR DISRUPTIVE CHILDREN

by

Cheryl Bodiford McNeil, Ph.D.
Toni Lynn Hembree-Kigin, Ph.D.
Sheila M. Eyberg, Ph.D.

The Center for Applied Psychology, Inc.
King of Prussia, Pennsylvania

SHORT-TERM PLAY THERAPY FOR DISRUPTIVE CHILDREN
by Cheryl Bodiford McNeil, Ph.D.
    Toni Lynn Hembree-Kigin, Ph.D.
    Sheila M. Eyberg, Ph.D.

Published by:
The Center for Applied Psychology, Inc.
P. O. Box 61587
King of Prussia, PA 19406 U.S.A.
Tel. 610/277-4020

The Center for Applied Psychology, Inc. is the publisher of Childswork/Childsplay, a catalog of products for mental health professionals, teachers and parents who wish to help children with their developmental, social and emotional growth. For a free catalog of books, games and toys to help children, call 1-800-962-1141.

ISBN 1-882732-51-0

Acknowledgments

We would like to thank the following individuals who provided helpful insights on early drafts of this manuscript: Alisa Bahl and Marsha Mills, Doctoral Students, Department of Psychology, West Virginia University, Morgantown; Dina Blacker, Assistant Clinical Director, Child Crisis Center, Mesa, Arizona; Dr. Gail Hashimoto, Child Psychotherapist, New York, NY; and Chanin Kennedy, Child Therapist, Morgantown, WV. We are indebted to Lawrence E. Shapiro, Ph.D., President, The Center for Applied Psychology, for his guidance and support through all stages of this project. A special thank you is also extended to Beth Ann Marcozzi, Marketing Representative, The Center for Applied Psychology, for keeping us on track with this manuscript. This book would not have been undertaken without the love and support of our families: Mom and Dad, Dolly and Danny McNeil, Grandma Curry, Grandma Lingerfelt, Jack, Debbie, Becky, Pete, Misty, and Amanda (CBM); Mom and Dad, Tim, Jon, and the Kigin clan (TLH-K); Mom, Dad, Bob, Connie, Feather, Bluebell, and Poosh (SME). We are especially grateful to Dr. Dan McNeil, Dr. Tim Kigin, and Dr. John Graham-Pole for their many sacrifices while we were secluded and immersed in writing. Finally, by challenging us to develop more effective play therapy procedures, many children and families dear to us have contributed to this work.

Table of Contents

Foreword

I once heard a therapist describe her job in a mental health agency as being like "cleaning a house with a toothbrush." This therapist, like most mental health workers today, was suffering the consequences of having too few resources, too large a caseload of children with too many problems, and too little time to help them.

To add to this dilemma, therapists and counselors have rarely been given the practical training to help children in the real world. The majority of clinicians have been taught non-directive "long-term" conceptual models of therapy, which assume that they have unlimited time and resources. Today, this is rarely the case, and professionals are looking at the kids they must treat and the exigencies of their jobs and wondering: "What can I do?"

Short-Term Play Therapy for Disruptive Children provides just the kind of answers that therapists and counselors are looking for. Cheryl Bodiford McNeil, Toni Hembree-Kigin, and Sheila Eyberg are seasoned professionals who have formulated a program based on years of clinical research and documented evidence of its effectiveness. The 12-session therapy described by the authors is unique in its combination and integration of therapeutic modalities and principles. Borrowing techniques from play therapy, cognitive and behavioral therapy, learning theory, and parent training, the authors have produced a program which is more than the sum of its parts.

Perhaps even more significantly, the authors have demonstrated the success of their model on really tough children: the ones who test our patience and our clinical skills, but comprise an estimated 50% of the clinical population. By stressing the need for both nurturant support and effective discipline, this model creates an opportunity for "difficult" children to get their intrapsychic needs met while their behavioral problems are immediately addressed.

While 12 hours of therapy may not seem like a lot to some clinicians, it is actually much more than most children get. Studies suggest that of the millions of children with significant emotional and behavioral problems, only a fraction of these get the help they need. It is my hope that this book will aid clinicians in every setting to deliver effective and professional services to the children who need them most.

– LAWRENCE E. SHAPIRO, Ph.D.
March 1996

1

FOUNDATIONS FOR
SHORT-TERM PLAY THERAPY
WITH DISRUPTIVE CHILDREN

It is four o'clock, and time to begin Jeremy's play therapy session. The therapist greets Jeremy and his mother in the waiting room. Jeremy says "Hi!" and begins running towards the playroom. The therapist makes a futile call for Jeremy to slow down, and quickly follows after him. Jeremy darts into the clinic director's office and begins rummaging through her desk. The therapist catches up with Jeremy and gently reminds him that it is time to go to the playroom. A giggling Jeremy crawls under the desk and in a sing-song voice chants, "You can't find me, na nanny boo boo." The therapist then patiently attempts to coax Jeremy out from under the desk by describing the fun toys in the therapy room. As she approaches from one side, Jeremy darts toward the door and runs into the playroom. When the therapist joins Jeremy in the therapy room, he is scaling the toy shelves and reaching for the graham crackers on top. She runs over to support him while saying, "I'm worried you'll get hurt. Would you please come down from there?" He yells, "Let go!" and leaps Ninja-style from the shelves to the bean bag chair. Jeremy unzips the bean bag chair, releasing a flood of styrofoam pellets. He backs up and slides into them, scattering pellets around the room. The therapist says, "You seem to have a lot of energy today. I'm wondering if you're upset about something." Jeremy responds by putting a handful of pellets in his mouth, spitting them at the therapist, and erupting in laughter. With a hint of irritation in her voice, the therapist says, "Now that's enough. You need to calm down." Jeremy yells, "Leave me alone!" and begins to scale the toy shelves again.

Active and disruptive children like Jeremy present numerous challenges for play therapists. It is hard to remain accepting and nurturing in the face of reckless, defiant, and frenetic behavior. In the above scenario, Jeremy's disruptive behavior made it difficult for the play therapist to adhere to Axlinian guidelines (see Table 1-1). Play therapy tenets which are in danger of being compromised with children like Jeremy include establishing and maintaining good rapport, accepting the child exactly as he or she is, maintaining a deep respect for the child's ability to solve his or her own problems, and not attempting to direct the child's actions or conversation in any manner (Axline, 1947).

In considering whether to attempt play therapy with children like Jeremy, a therapist must first assess the goals of treatment. Play therapy is likely to be the treatment of choice if the primary goal is to help the disruptive child cope with adjustment issues or trauma such as death of a family member, sexual abuse, physical abuse, natural disaster, terminal illness, divorce, and witnessing violence. On the other hand, if the primary goal is to produce rapid behavioral improvements, it may be best to offer parent training, problem-solving skills training, strategic family therapy, or social skills training. These therapies have been shown to be effective interventions, improving compliance, disruptive behavior, peer interaction skills, and familial relationships in a short time frame (e.g., Kazdin, 1988; Lyman & Hembree-Kigin, 1994;

Mash & Barkley, 1989; Schroeder & Gordon, 1991; Walker & Roberts, 1992). There also are situational factors that make play therapy either the treatment of choice for a disruptive child or a valuable adjunctive intervention. Individual play therapy is often indicated when care-givers are unavailable to participate in treatment. Examples include children with acting-out behavior who are in residential or day treatment placements, in foster care, or receiving school-based counseling. Play therapy also is appropriate for disruptive children whose parents are unable to participate effectively in therapy due to mental or physical illness, intellectual limitations, and/or dealing with multiple life crises.

Table 1-1. Axlinian Principles for Nondirective Play Therapy

---

1. The therapist must develop a warm, friendly relationship with the child, in which good rapport is established as soon as possible.

2. The therapist accepts the child exactly as he or she is.

3. The therapist establishes a feeling of permissiveness in the relationship so that the child feels free to express his or her feelings completely.

4. The therapist is alert to recognize the feelings the child is expressing and reflects those feelings back to help the child gain insight into his or her behavior.

5. The therapist maintains a deep respect for the child's ability to solve his or her own problems if given an opportunity to do so. It is the child's responsibility to make choices and institute change.

6. The therapist does not attempt to direct the child's actions or conversation in any manner. The child leads the way; the therapist follows.

7. The therapist does not attempt to hurry the therapy along. It is a gradual process and is recognized as such by the therapist.

8. The therapist establishes only those limitations that are necessary to anchor the therapy to the world of reality and to make the child aware of his or her responsibility in the relationship.

Adapted from Axline (1947).

Having chosen to conduct play therapy with an acting-out child, therapists are faced not only with the clinical challenges of this population, but also with the business demands inherent in a competitive marketplace. Managed care guidelines require quality assurance and time-limit-ed treatment. Put simply, managed care dictates that mental health professionals "do more with less." Treatment goals are required to be defined precisely and to be linked clearly to presenting complaints. Progress must be measurable and assessed both during and after treatment. On average, approved interventions are limited to 6 to 12 sessions. With children like Jeremy, therapist attempts to deal with disruptive behaviors can consume a great portion of each therapy hour. Whereas disruptive behavior can be "worked through" in longer-term therapies, there is insufficient time for this process in short-term play therapy approaches.

From a psychodynamic perspective, Sloves and Peterlin (1993) have discussed the need to institute fundamental changes in traditional play therapy to obtain success in a time-limited format:

> In important ways this method goes against the grain of several prevailing models of Axlinian/Rogerian play therapy. The therapist is sympathetic, friendly, and empathic, but rarely permissive in the relationship. While the therapist respects children's ability to solve problems, it seems unfair to let them do it in their own time, especially when the therapist possesses the collective knowledge of other children who, in similar circumstances, have confronted similar problems. The therapist, as ally, does everything to hurry the therapy along without frightening the child into passivity, active resistance, or flight. The therapist guides the child while maintaining the positive transference in the face of a constantly threatening negative transference. (p. 304)

We agree with Sloves and Peterlin's premise that major changes are necessary to adapt traditional play therapy to a short-term format. However, a major theoretical divergence is our focus on the integration of behavioral principles with traditional concerns (Eyberg, 1988).

We recognize that it is counterintuitive to combine such disparate orientations, conjuring up the image of mixing oil and water. Yet, our reasoning is more understandable in the context of our clinical training and experiences. We have been trained in both traditional play therapy and behavioral methods, finding merit in each of these approaches. Our experience in traditional play therapy has taught us that there is important therapeutic value in allowing the child to lead the play, and that nondirective play therapy is an expedient vehicle for forming a powerful alliance. We recognize that therapist factors such as warmth and unconditional positive regard help children to accept their true selves and feel safe in processing threatening material. We also find great merit in behavioral and cognitive-behavioral methods (e.g., Knell, 1993) such as those described in Table 1-2.

From a behavioral perspective, problems are approached by considering their antecedents and consequences. In this way, aspects of the environment that set the child up for failure can be altered, with both social and tangible reinforcement used to increase desirable behaviors. Certain behaviors are promoted while others are discouraged through the use of differential attention. When teaching children new skills such as relaxation and social problem-solving, the skills are broken down into their components, each step is modeled, and skill usage is prompted and reinforced. For fearful and anxious children, systematic desensitization can be employed to expose children gradually to anxiety-arousing stimuli. But most importantly, behavioral and cognitive-behavioral interventions can produce rapid, measurable change that can be readily observed by others and documented for managed care agencies.

We are not the only clinicians to recognize the potential value of integrating traditional play therapy with behaviorally-oriented methods. In describing Cognitive-Behavioral Play Therapy (CBPT), Knell (1993) outlined six characteristic features:

1. CBPT involves the child in treatment via play.

2. CBPT focuses on the child's thoughts, feelings, fantasies, and environment.

3. CBPT provides a strategy or strategies for developing more adaptive thoughts and behaviors.

4. CBPT is structured, directive, and goal-oriented, rather than open-ended.

5. CBPT incorporates empirically-demonstrated techniques.

6. CBPT allows for an empirical examination of treatment. (pp. 44-45)

We consider these properties to be descriptive of our own approach to integrating behavioral methods and traditional play therapy as well. Yet, we diverge from CBPT in two important ways. First, our treatment program is designed specifically for children with disruptive behavior. It includes structural features and techniques that can make play therapy more effective when working with this difficult population. And second, our approach is designed to accomplish circumscribed goals in a short-term, 12-session format. This allows us to work within the time constraints imposed by managed care.

To accomplish specific goals in a short time span, we have found it necessary to structure play therapy to maximize productivity. We have adapted traditional play therapy so that about half of each session is devoted to task-oriented activities, and the other half is reserved for child-directed play. Activities such as therapeutic games, role-play, thematic drawings, educational workbooks, and dramatic play are used to address circumscribed goals during the first half of each session. The second child-directed play portion is incorporated to address attachment issues, provide a safe forum for working through difficult material, enhance self-esteem, and increase motivation and cooperation with task-oriented activities.

To be efficient in accomplishing circumscribed goals in short-term therapy, a conceptual shift must be made in how one thinks about disruptive behavior. In traditional long-term play therapy, disruptive behavior has been conceptualized as rich clinical material. However, in short-term play therapy, it is considered an impediment to treatment progress. Sloves and Peterlin (1993) make this argument from a psychoanalytic perspective:

> In long-term treatment, the therapist expects some regression and, in some instances, encourages it because there are few limitations placed on the "working through" process. The opposite is true in brief treatment. Here, technique limits the child's dependence and regression. In psychoanalytic terms, the therapist actively thwarts development of a transference neurosis. The therapist consistently and firmly maintains the focus on adaptation and conflict resolution. (p. 303)

From a behavioral play therapy perspective, off-task and oppositional behaviors make treatment inefficient. Children who are engaged in disruptive (i.e., "regressive") behavior are not able to focus their energy on working toward circumscribed therapeutic goals. Similarly, therapists who are dealing with escalating behavior problems will have difficulty eliciting cooperation with goal-directed activities. Disruptive behavior also can compromise therapist-child rapport. Thus, a priority of short-term play therapy with acting-out children is the prevention and effective management of disruptive and off-task behavior.

Contingent attention is arguably the most powerful strategy available for dealing with disruptive behavior and is a central feature of our behavioral play therapy approach. Use of contingent attention stems from the knowledge that children are rewarded by attention. Disruptive children are particularly skillful at obtaining attention through negative behaviors such as whining, talking back, and running away. There are at least two ways in which a negative attention-seeking pattern can develop. Some children have learning histories in which their prosocial behaviors were largely ignored, while their inappropriate behaviors received intense attention in the form of scolding, nagging, and yelling. Thus, they learned to engage in high-

Table 1-2. Behavioral and Cognitive-Behavioral Techniques

Technique	Example
Systematic Desensitization	A dog phobic is gradually exposed to steps on a fear hierarchy (e.g., stuffed dog, puppy, small dog at a distance) while in a relaxed state.
Positive Reinforcement	Child receives praise and a sticker for rehearsal of skills (e.g., ignoring teasing, identifying feelings).
Shaping	A child with Selective Mutism is reinforced for successive approximations toward conversation (e.g., speaking to a parent in the therapist's presence, speaking to the therapist in parent's presence, speaking to therapist when alone).
Differential Reinforcement of Other Behavior (DRO)	When a resistant child expresses boredom with a book about stepfamilies, the therapist ignores the comment and continues reading aloud. When the child remarks about a picture in the book, the therapist reinforces on-task behavior by enthusiastically showing interest in the child's comment.
Modeling	While coloring with an overly perfectionistic child, the therapist marks outside the lines and then models a coping statement, such as "That's okay. Everybody colors outside the lines once in a while. My picture is still pretty."
Self-Monitoring	A preschooler colors a square on a chart each time she wakes up in the morning with dry sheets.
Recording Dysfunctional Thoughts	A child with low self-esteem uses a tape recorder to record every time he says, "I can't. . ."
Confronting Irrational Beliefs	A child describes a scenario in which he asks a girl to play and she declines. He expresses the irrational belief that she declined to play with him because she does not like him. The therapist uses a hypothesis testing approach to help the child generate alternative plausible explanations (e.g., she had to do her homework).
Bibliotherapy	In therapy with a sexual abuse survivor, the therapist uses published books on sexual abuse and works with the child to create an individualized story about the child's own experiences that emphasizes positive coping strategies.

rate and negative behaviors to satisfy their attentional needs. Others have unusually strong needs for stimulation and are gratified by the arousing nature of negative attention. Recognizing the power of attention, play therapists can use their attention selectively to encourage some behaviors while discouraging others.

To enhance efficiency, behaviors that contribute to work productivity are attended to systematically. Good work behaviors may include sitting still, looking at the therapist, answering questions, staying in the playroom, playing gently with materials, and putting forth effort. Positive attention can be provided in a variety of ways. The therapist can provide specific praise for desirable behaviors, describe what the child is doing well, imitate appropriate behaviors, reflect relevant verbalizations, and interpret thematic content. Efficiency also is enhanced by withdrawing attention from behaviors that interfere with work productivity. Examples of nonproductive behaviors include rolling around the room, yelling, taunting the therapist, hiding therapeutic materials, and being off-task. After explaining in advance that these behaviors will be ignored, the therapist systematically withdraws attention for nonproductive activities and looks for the first opportunity to attend selectively to an alternative, appropriate behavior. Through contingent attention, the therapist can gently guide the child's behavior in a positive direction, preventing minor disruptive or off-task behaviors from escalating.

In addition to the emphasis on managing disruptive behavior, developing a treatment plan is fundamental to achieving efficiency in our short-term play therapy approach. Based on information obtained during an intake evaluation, we develop circumscribed and measurable treatment goals. We remain cognizant of the limitations inherent in a short-term format. We do not expect to address all of the problems that a child may present. Instead, we prioritize and focus effort on a small number (three or fewer) of obtainable treatment goals. Examples of goals that might be identified in our treatment plans include (a) improvement of peer interactional skills; (b) the ability to use words instead of disruptive behavior to express sadness, anger, or frustration; (c) the ability to use relaxation skills to reduce anxiety; (d) decreased sexualized behavior; and (e) improved mood. To accomplish these goals, we devise discrete objectives for each session. The objectives are designed to build upon one another to ultimately accomplish larger treatment goals. They also enhance therapist efficiency by ensuring that goal-oriented work is accomplished in each session. In addition to enhancing efficiency, incorporation of session objectives and treatment goals facilitates the evaluation of treatment progress and outcome, an essential component of quality assurance in a managed care environment.

Book Overview

In this text, we present a short-term play therapy approach for disruptive children that integrates traditional and behavioral concerns. Emphasis is placed on maximizing productivity and efficiency in each and every session. One way in which this is accomplished is through structuring the session so that a portion is always spent in planned, task-oriented activities. A second method of maximizing efficiency is to employ powerful behavior management strategies to prevent disruptive behavior from interfering with work productivity. Finally, session objectives and treatment goals are carefully articulated so that valuable session time is not wasted and outcome can be evaluated.

This book begins with a description of how to structure play therapy sessions into portions for (a) checking in with caregivers, (b) conducting therapist-directed activities, (c) conducting child-directed play therapy, and (d) checking out with caregivers by reviewing therapeutic progress and assigning homework. In structuring play therapy sessions, emphasis is placed on the importance of establishing routines and precedents. Next, we provide chapters detailing the play therapy process skills and behavior management techniques. Among others, these include praise, descriptive statements, reflection, imitation, questions, interpretation, reinforcers, strategic ignoring and contingent attention, giving effective directions, and rules for being a good listener. Five chapters are devoted to a chronological presentation of our 12-session model. A summary of the procedures used in the 12-session model is presented in Table 1-3. In our final chapter, we revisit the case of "Jeremy." We follow Jeremy's treatment from the initial session to termination, illustrating how to manage his disruptive behavior while working toward short-term play therapy goals. We recommend a careful reading of this final chapter as it integrates key concepts using rich clinical detail.

Table 1-3. A 12-Session Model for Short-Term Play Therapy

Session(s)	Procedures
1 - 2	Review consent/confidentiality Educate parents regarding play therapy Explain and model play therapy structure for child Devise a therapy contract Use pretreatment assessment to devise a treatment plan and goals
3 - 8	Conduct individual play therapy with child using Child's Work/Child's Play structure Assign homework to enhance progress toward play therapy goals
8 - 11	Begin termination process by increasing parental involvement in therapy and decreasing child dependency on therapist Coach parents in use of play therapy skills Assign homework so that parents provide daily play therapy sessions at home
12	Post-treatment assessment Review progress toward treatment goals Termination party

2

STRUCTURING THE PLAY THERAPY SESSION

When doing short-term play therapy with disruptive children, we have found it beneficial to structure the therapy hour carefully. Otherwise, high-rate behaviors such as jumping on furniture, searching through the therapist's desk, screeching, and running out of the therapy room can interfere with the therapeutic process. Often these behaviors can be prevented or minimized by providing children with predictable routines, clear limits, and transition rituals. Thus, we have added more structure to the traditional play therapy session in order to be more efficient in working with disruptive children.

Dividing the Therapy Session into "Child's Work" and "Child's Play"

In our approach, the therapy hour is divided into a therapist-directed portion, called "Child's Work," followed by a child-directed portion, called "Child's Play." We incorporated a Child's Work portion into each play therapy hour in response to managed care efficiency guidelines. To be competitive in obtaining third-party reimbursement, therapists must accomplish circumscribed goals in fewer than 12 sessions. We no longer have the luxury of allowing children to bring issues into therapy at their own pace, over many sessions. Thus, our short-term therapy approach includes Child's Work as a method for speeding up the therapeutic process by establishing a focus upon specific themes and issues. Child's Work incorporates planned activities that address pre-established therapeutic goals. Examples of Child's Work activities include therapeutic games, role-play, presentation of educational material, and thematic drawings. As seasoned play therapists, we know that children have a remarkable capacity to work through conflict when engaged in a safe, nurturing, and accepting relationship with a therapist. Child's Play was included in this short-term intervention to preserve both the "heart and art" of traditional play therapy. In Child's Play, the child is allowed to select the play activities, and the therapist uses child-directed play therapy skills to form a strong interpersonal bond. The medium of child-directed play is used to facilitate communication at the child's developmental level.

Conducting Child's Work Before Child's Play

There are several reasons for having Child's Work always precede Child's Play. From a practical perspective, disruptive children will be more cooperative with planned activities when they know that "free play" will follow. In contrast, if active children are permitted to begin sessions with free play, it is difficult to transition them to a structured activity chosen by the therapist. For example, suppose that a hyperactive and oppositional child begins the session by building a fort with blocks. Then the therapist says, "I have an activity that I would like for us to do. Please come over here and draw a picture of your family doing something together." The child is likely to refuse, leading the therapist to either abandon the planned activity or take on the role of disciplinarian. When "work" time always comes before "play" time, such transitions are avoided, and children quickly adapt to the set routine.

In addition to practical constraints, there are also therapeutic benefits to having Child's Work precede Child's Play. By beginning with thematic activities, conflictual issues and emotional responses can be triggered early in the session. The child then is likely to carry these themes over into the Child's Play portion of the session, providing rich, therapeutic material for nondirective play therapy. It also allows ample time for the child to work through strong affect and reactivate defenses before leaving the session. A final therapeutic benefit of doing work before play is that the session is ended on a fun and positive note. This helps the child to look forward to the next therapy session.

Allocating Play Therapy Time

Because we believe that caregivers can be important allies in play therapy, parental "Check-In" and "Check-Out" times are included at the beginning and end of each session. To protect the integrity of the child's individual therapy time, the Check-In and Check-Out times are usually kept brief, approximately 10 minutes each. This leaves approximately 20 minutes to devote to Child's Work and 20 minutes for Child's Play. These times must be flexible for a variety of reasons. For example, a particular planned activity for Child's Work may require more than 20 minutes, leaving less time for Child's Play. Alternatively, a child may not be ready to work in a particular therapy session due to fatigue, extreme restlessness, or a traumatic prior event. In such cases, the therapist may choose to shorten the Child's Work portion. Occasionally, the Check-In or Check-Out time may need to be extended to address crises or to communicate with parents regarding complex issues. As a general principle, however, therapists should attempt to structure therapy sessions in accordance with the time allocations outlined previously.

Importance of Routine and Predictability

Maintaining a predictable play therapy routine is important for all children. It helps them to feel safe and reduces anxiety. Routine and predictability are even more critical when working with children who engage in disruptive behavior. Minor changes in routine can cause these children to become overstimulated, resulting in such behaviors as leaving the area without permission, uncontrolled laughter, motor restlessness, failure to follow directions, and touching off-limits materials. The routine should be clearly established in the first session, thereby setting the precedent for subsequent sessions. It is all too easy to set potentially problematic precedents at the beginning of therapy. For example, if the child is allowed to run from the playroom to the waiting area unescorted, the therapist will have a difficult time teaching the child to transition calmly in later sessions. Therapists who allow children to choose the therapy toys from a cabinet will encounter resistance later when attempting to select the toys themselves. If a snack or a treat is given to the child during the intake appointment, the child will likely expect/demand a treat at each visit. While giving a treat can be therapeutic (e.g., as a symbol of nurturance with neglected children), it can become a source of conflict if not routinely provided. Other events that can set problematic precedents include bathroom and water breaks during therapy time, visiting parents in the waiting area, and failing to clean up toys. A number of behavior problems can be prevented by establishing a routine at the outset and sticking to it.

Setting Up the Playroom for Success

Calm and cooperative children can function well in a stimulating playroom that includes such materials as a sand tray, water table, pretend kitchen, working sink, paint easel, and open shelves of visible toys. Children with behavioral problems, however, quickly become overstimulated and disruptive in such an environment. Inattentive and active children are easily distracted by a large selection of toys and games. They frequently switch activities in a disorganized, impulsive fashion. Not only does this cause them to have difficulty listening to the therapist, but also it prevents them from staying with an activity long enough to do in-depth work and derive therapeutic benefit. In addition, an overstimulated child's behavior often escalates to throwing toys, climbing on shelves, or yelling. This type of rough and destructive activity interferes with the therapy process by diminishing rapport and taking time away from more constructive pursuits.

Child-proofing is the first step toward setting up a successful playroom for children with disruptive behavior problems. This involves securing and/or removing potentially dangerous objects such as electrical outlets, thumbtacks, radiators, unstable shelves or file cabinets, windows, and cords of blinds. Valuables which can be damaged should be removed as well. Examples include electronic equipment, framed pictures, telephones, and potted plants. The second step is to remove objects and materials that are potentially distracting (e.g., shelves of visible toys, chairs with casters) or inappropriate for use during play therapy sessions (see Child's Play Section of this chapter for additional information addressing toy selection). In general, the best playroom for children with disruptive behavior problems is one which contains nothing but a child-sized table and chairs, bright decorative designs painted on the walls, and the toys and materials needed for that particular portion of the session. This structured environment eliminates many of the extraneous behavior problems that impede therapeutic progress.

Check-In with Caregiver(s)

Each play session begins with a Check-In time with the parents. In most cases, the child is present during the Check-In time. It is helpful to include the child for several reasons: (a) if excluded from this time, the child can become concerned that the therapist is revealing confidences or expressing disapproval, thereby undermining trust; (b) the child can be a productive participant; and (c) close supervision is needed for children with disruptive behavior problems, and often there is no qualified adult available. Parents are reminded that an alternative arrangement can be made if they wish to speak with the therapist privately.

The purpose of the Check-In time is to provide parents and children with the opportunity to share information that might contribute to the therapeutic process. They are asked about problems that have occurred during the week, as well as familial stressors and significant events. As many parents have a tendency to vent frustration, they often must be prompted by the therapist to share positive observations in addition to negative ones. It also is important to be directive in setting time limits. We tell parents, "Because Susie's play therapy time is so valuable, we will need to make sure that our Check-In time does not extend longer than 10 minutes." For parents who want to talk longer than the allotted time, we explain that we need to get started with their child's therapy and will have the chance to talk more at the end of the session.

With the child present, it is important to have a few toys in the Check-In room that can entertain the child and minimize time-consuming disruptive behaviors. Although these toys enhance Check-In, they can serve as distractors during subsequent Child's Work. Thus, it is optimal for the Check-In to be conducted in a room separate from the playroom. With acting-out children, we have found it easier to escort them from the Check-In room to the playroom that is set up for Child's Work than to take away toys with which they are already engaged. For children who have difficulty staying in the Check-In room, we have found it helpful to conduct Check-In with our bodies positioned in front of the door. This strategy discourages impulsive and repetitive attempts to run out of the room.

Child's Work

To enhance cooperation with therapist-directed activities, the playroom should contain only those materials being used for planned Child's Work activities. In the first session, it is advisable to set the precedent that the child will always walk alongside the therapist from the Check-In room to the playroom. For children who attempt to run ahead of the therapist, we recommend asking them to come back and walk alongside of the therapist. Otherwise, the disruptive child will learn that it is acceptable to run around the clinic unescorted. By observing the same walking rituals each session, children will adapt to the structure, increasing the likelihood that they will enter the playroom calmly and ready to work. As previously suggested, therapists can actively discourage children from leaving the playroom without permission by positioning themselves in front of the door during Child's Work.

We begin Child's Work by reminding children of the playroom rules. They are told that they must stay in the playroom, play gently with the toys and materials, and not do anything that will endanger themselves or the therapist. Children also are reminded of the structure of the session. They are told that we always do our work before our play. Even though we use the term "work" to refer to therapist-directed activities, fun aspects of those activities also are emphasized. In explaining the rules and structure of the session, the therapist might say,

> Just like always, we need to remember our playroom rules. First, you need to stay right here with me in the playroom. Second, you need to take good care of my toys by playing very gently with them. Third, it is important that everybody stays safe. So, no hitting, climbing, or throwing is allowed. Wow! You are being a great listener. I think I'll give you a hand stamp for showing me your good listening skills. Now, remember that we always do our work before our play. First we are going to do some things that I picked out. Most of these things will be fun, but you might feel lots of different ways. Sometimes you might feel happy, and sometimes you might feel sad or angry. (For older children, you may substitute words like "embarrassed" or "anxious.") All feelings are okay,

and this is a safe place to talk about feelings. Thanks for being a good listener. Here's a fun game that I brought for us to play today.

Because each child enters therapy with a unique set of issues and therapeutic goals, the specific activities used during Child's Work must be individualized on a case-by-case basis. This flexible approach allows therapists to draw upon their unique strengths, experiences, and training in choosing activities for Child's Work. Some therapists may prefer to design their own activities, role-play, and materials, while others may prefer to select from a variety of commercially-available therapy products. Most of these products are available through therapeutic catalogs such as Childswork/Childsplay (1-800-962-1141).

There is an endless array of therapeutic activities that can be used to address the individualized goals of Child's Work. For example, we have used audiotaping and videotaping to stimulate the interest of children while rehearsing communications skills. A puppet theater can serve as a nonthreatening vehicle for discussing traumatic events. Similarly, children may use projective drawings to explore material too threatening to verbalize directly. When dealing with family issues, doll houses are excellent tools for promoting symbolic play. For children who are unable or unprepared to communicate directly with significant others (e.g., because of death, incarceration, or abuse), letter writing and pretend telephone calls can provide a safe medium for expressing thoughts and feelings. Self-esteem issues can be addressed by having a child construct and illustrate a book called *What I Like About Me!* These are but a few examples of the kinds of activities that may be used during Child's Work. Regardless of the particular activity selected, Child's Work should be engaging and capture the imagination and attention of disruptive children who may be resistant to therapist-directed activities.

When choosing Child's Work activities, the therapist should attempt to promote cross-setting generalization. One way that this can be accomplished is to maximize the similarity between the clinic setting and the real-life setting in which problems are displayed. For example, consider the case of a child who has difficulty falling asleep at night because of anxiety-arousing thoughts. To enhance generalization, the play therapist and child may set up the playroom to simulate the child's bedroom (e.g., put cushions on floor, dim lights) during Child's Work. In this setting, the child can rehearse relaxation and the use of positive imagery. For a child who has difficulty concentrating at school, a pretend classroom can be set up in the playroom. During Child's Work, the child can practice voluntarily going to a "quiet desk" when distracted by others. Similarly, generalization of skills for testifying in court is more likely to occur when the playroom is set up to resemble a courtroom. In Child's Work, children can be taught to reduce their anxiety by focusing on a nonthreatening object or person in the pretend courtroom such as a doll placed on the attorney's desk, a parent, or an empty chair. Because it is unlikely that generalization will occur without direct programming, we encourage therapists to be creative in devising Child's Work activities that simulate real-life situations.

Regardless of the type of Child's Work activity selected, there will occasionally be times when a child is not prepared to work in therapy. When adults do not feel like making good use of therapy time, they have the resources needed to call in "sick" or reschedule the appointment. Children often are brought to therapy whether or not they are capable of working. They may enter therapy hungry, tired, distracted by the first snow of the season, ill, distressed by a recent argument with a parent, or wound up from a birthday party they just left. In such cases, it is tempting to suspend the work altogether and move directly to Child's Play. We recommend, however, that the therapist always maintain the Child's Work - Child's Play sequence of therapy. This can be accomplished by devoting only a minimal amount of time to Child's Work and adapting the work so as to set up the child for success (e.g., instead of asking the child to design a card for his incarcerated father, the activity can be reduced to producing a simple drawing). The purpose of maintaining the therapy sequence is to avoid setting a precedent that it is acceptable for children not to work. If the routine is broken, valuable play therapy time may be lost in subsequent sessions as children attempt to negotiate their way out of Child's Work.

Transitioning from Child's Work to Child's Play

Approximately five minutes before the end of Child's Work, a transition statement should be given such as, "In just a little while, it will be time to take a break." When the Child's Work portion is completed, the child should be given the opportunity to take a bathroom break and get a drink of water. By having this break occur at the same point in every session, children will request fewer breaks during therapy time. During this break, the therapist brings a preselected set of Child's Play toys to the playroom. Many times, the child will obviously be enjoying the Child's Work activity and want to continue it without a break. We recommend that a break still be taken to maintain the routine of the therapy structure. After the break, the child can choose from the selected toys or can choose to continue the Child's Work activity. If the break is omitted, precious therapy time in subsequent sessions may have to be devoted to re-teaching the structure of therapy to the child.

Child's Play

In Child's Play, the therapist follows the child's lead and provides a supportive atmosphere in which the child can work through difficult issues. A primary goal of this portion of play therapy is to build a strong relationship between the therapist and child. Through this relationship, children are nurtured and provided with emotionally corrective experiences. When conducting short-term therapies, rapport must be established quickly to motivate children to work hard and cooperate with therapist-directed activities. A second important goal of Child's Play is to build self-esteem. Children with disruptive behavior are frequently the targets of adult and peer criticism, which can take a toll on their self-esteem. This undermines their confidence in solving problems, taking emotional risks, and handling conflict. A third goal of Child's Play is to improve communications and social skills. Skill enhancement can empower children to cope more effectively with interpersonal problems by expressing desires and feelings through appropriate verbal communication.

Careful selection of Child's Play toys facilitates progress toward therapeutic goals. Toys are chosen to promote mastery experiences, communication, and prosocial behavior. Mastery is encouraged by the use of construction toys that match or are slightly below the child's developmental level. Examples include building blocks, magnet boards, Tinker Toys, waffle blocks, and Erector sets. Constructional toys allow for many small accomplishments (e.g., fitting two blocks together), and there are few "wrong" ways to play with them that would lead to a sense of failure. Because board games have winners and losers and encourage competition, they are typically excluded from Child's Play.

Communication between the therapist and child is promoted through the use of toys that are designed for pretend and symbolic play. Examples include doll houses, puppet theaters, telephones, zoo and farm sets, tea and cooking sets, modeling clay, crayons and paper, and costumes. These toys stimulate child conversation about salient feelings, ideas, and opinions. Conversely, toys and activities that are avoided during Child's Play because they inhibit child communication include musical instruments, board games, hide-and-seek, and singing.

With children who have disruptive behavior problems, it is important to set them up for prosocial behavior during Child's Play. Certain toys and activities should be avoided because they stimulate active, destructive, rambunctious, or aggressive play. This type of play impedes the therapeutic goals by causing the therapist to have to set limits, thereby placing emotional distance between the therapist and child. It is also difficult to discuss sensitive material while running and jumping. We recommend excluding the following categories of toys and activities when working with disruptive children: sports equipment (e.g., sponge footballs, baseball bats, boxing gloves, basketball hoops); weapon play (e.g., sword fights, cowboys and Indians, super-heros, martial arts); and "messy" toys that require frequent limit-setting (e.g., sand boxes, water tables, paints, glue).

Transitioning from Child's Play to Check-Out

Disruptive children often have a difficult time ending Child's Play. They may attempt to bar-gain for more time (e.g., "Just let me finish this picture.") or confront the therapist (e.g., "You promised we could play with clay!"). Although it might seem harmless to allow Child's Play to be extended for a few extra minutes, it gives children the message that time rules are nego-tiable, and it sets a problematic precedent. When it comes to enforcing rules such as those designed to protect the children's safety or the frame of therapy, it is better for a therapist to be more like a "brick wall" than a "rubber band." If disruptive children are allowed to stretch the limits, they are encouraged to engage the therapist in power struggles, thereby compro-mising therapeutic efficiency and rapport.

We feel that it is optimal to end the Child's Play portion of the session by having children assist in cleaning up. This helps to instill a sense of personal responsibility and is consistent with the clean-up expectations held in other settings. Problems ending Child's Play can be minimized by having an end-of-session ritual. Approximately five minutes before the end of Child's Play, the child is given a transition statement like, "In just a few minutes, it will be time to stop playing and clean up."

Children can be motivated to end the session cooperatively and to clean up the playroom by ensuring that a rewarding activity always follows. Examples of possible rewards include: put a penny in a gumball machine, bounce a special ball on the way to the Check-Out room, choose a prize out of the big magic hat, add a sticker to the sticker chart and show it to mom, or sing a song with the therapist during the walk to the Check-Out room. From the first ses-sion, a precedent is set by telling the child, "It's time for playtime to be over now, and the toys need to be put away. My rule is that if you help me pick up the toys, you will get to... [choose a good behavior prize from the big purple hat.]" Sometimes the ending ritual can be enhanced by singing a clean-up song or playing special clean-up music.

Check-Out

Just as children are taught to walk alongside the therapist as they move from the Check-In room to the playroom, they should be encouraged to walk appropriately from the playroom back to the room where the caregiver(s) is waiting. Children are included in the Check-Out portion of the session to allay any fears that they may have that confidences will be breached. Also, they can be valuable contributors to the Check-Out review of treatment progress.

One of the important goals of the Check-Out time is to communicate to parents the therapeutic nature of the play therapy work. When parents are given insufficient information about the work being accomplished in therapy, they must rely on their child's account of what happened during the session. It is common for children to report that they "played and had fun," leading parents to question the value of therapy. To keep parents invested in their child's therapy, they are informed in general terms about the work that was accomplished in each session.

The child's right to confidentiality must always be balanced with the parents' need to know about the content of therapy. Thus, at the end of the Child's Play portion, the therapist and child discuss what material should be shared with the parents during the Check-out period. Sensitive information regarding the child's feelings and thoughts typically is not shared with the parents. Occasionally, the child may reveal a sensitive issue that the therapist feels would be beneficial for the parents to know about. In such cases, the child's permission is obtained before sharing that information with parents. The following is an example of a therapist preparing a child for the Check-Out period:

> Rachel, it is almost time for us to go to meet with your mom and dad. We talked about some really important things today. I was really happy that you told me about your fears that your mom and dad might get a divorce. A lot of children worry about that when they hear their parents arguing like you did last night. You were brave to tell me about that. I think that it is important for your mom and dad to know that you are worried. I would like for you and I to talk to them about the fight when we meet with them in a few minutes. Does that sound okay to you? [Rachel nods affirmatively.] Is there anything that you don't want me to talk to your parents about? [Rachel shakes her head no.] Okay. I think you'll feel better after we talk to your parents about this.

In addition to communicating therapeutic progress to parents, another important goal of Check-Out is to promote generalization of treatment gains. One way that this can be accomplished is to involve parents and other caregivers as allies in the treatment process. Through homework assignments, caregivers can prompt and reinforce skills acquired during Child's Work. In the case of a child who is having difficulty falling asleep at night, for example, the mother could be given a homework assignment consisting of three components: (a) dimming the bedroom lights, (b) prompting the child to imagine being in her "happy place," and (c) playing a recorded relaxation tape. Other examples of homework assignments that can support play therapy goals and enhance generalization are listed in Table 2-1.

Table 2-1. Homework Assignments for Reinforcing Child's Work Goals

Child's Work Goal	Homework Assignment
Identifying feelings	Prompt child to label both positive and negative feelings
Saying "I feel angry when. . ." instead of acting out anger	Prompt child to use feeling words during conflicts with peers and siblings
Recognizing accomplishments	Before bedtime, have child list five things he or she did well that day
Promoting attachment	Spend five minutes a day in child-directed play
Expressing anger through acceptable channels	Prompt and reinforce the following ways of expressing anger: hitting a pillow, scribbling on a piece of paper really hard, writing an angry letter and tearing it up
Reducing anxiety	Play a relaxation tape for child before bedtime
Reducing public masturbation	Restrict masturbation to private settings
Improving listening skills	Prompt and reinforce good listening skills
Increasing impulse control	Prompt and reinforce use of self-control strategies
Increasing sharing with peers	Rehearse sharing before dropping child off at daycare/school, and discuss targeted skill with teacher

3

PLAY THERAPY PROCESS SKILLS

Play therapy process skills (e.g., Axline, 1947; O'Connor & Schaefer, 1994; Schaefer & O'Connor, 1983) are used in interactions with children throughout each therapy session, including the Check-In and Check-Out times. We use these skills selectively to guide children to be productive play therapy participants. In short-term play therapy, we attend to child behaviors and verbalizations that promote progress toward session objectives and overall treatment goals, while redirecting those that are extraneous or counterproductive. The process skills are used selectively to promote good listening, verbalization of thoughts and feelings, cooperation, staying on task, putting forth good effort, and complying with playroom rules. The process skills also promote child confidence and self-esteem, as well as a strong therapist-child relationship that is characterized by mutual like, respect, trust, and communication. Specific process skills described in this chapter are description, reflection, praise, questions, interpretation, and imitation.

Description

Definition and Examples. A description is a nonevaluative comment that usually addresses the behavior of the child, but may also describe the child's appearance or demeanor, therapist's thoughts or feelings, or toys/therapeutic materials. Descriptions provide a verbal picture of the present situation. Commonly, descriptions are used to provide a running commentary on the activity of the child in the therapy room. Examples of descriptive statements include:

> *"This morning you're sitting down while you draw the picture of your family."*
> *"You're in your chair with your hands in your lap. I think you're ready for the first card."*
> *"You're drawing those windows slowly and carefully."*
> *"I see you have a lot of stickers on your shirt."*
> *"You look like you're thinking hard about what I said."*
> *"The doll is helping his father with the work, just like you help your father."*
> *"The horse is sharing his hay with the pig."*
> *"You're using your 'I feel...' statements."*
> *"You are looking closely at the pictures in this book and paying attention to the story."*

Rationale. Describing builds a child's self confidence. By carefully watching and commenting on what the child is doing, the therapist communicates that the child's activities are interesting and important to the therapist. This message leads the child to recognize the value of his or her choices and ideas. Disruptive children are often careless with toys and other objects and bring to therapy a history of criticism related to constructional tasks. Because the play therapy setting is designed to promote working with such tasks, the therapist has many opportunities to attend to incompatible play behaviors (e.g., playing calmly, planning ahead). A simple description focused on the child's product, such as "I see you're getting the roof lined up to finish that sturdy log cabin," can begin a process wherein disruptive children begin to change their negative self perceptions.

Describing also enhances problem-solving skills. The therapist can use descriptions to point out effective problem-solving strategies and encourage the child's persistence. For a child who has difficulty handling frustration, the therapist can say, "You turned it all different ways to figure out how it fits. It's hard to get it to fit, but you aren't giving up." When the therapist describes the child's attempts to solve a problem, positive attention is being provided for task persistence. Children stay with the task for longer periods, thus increasing the likelihood of successful problem-solving.

Describing improves the child's attention span. Disruptive children may be distractible and have difficulty attending to a task or game for more than a few minutes. Describing adds interest value to an activity and helps children to stay with it for longer periods. By frequently describing children's behaviors during Child's Work and Child's Play, the therapist teaches children to think about their actions in words. Just as the therapist's words hold the child's attention to the task, eventually the child's "silent descriptions" will serve the same function during independent activities.

Describing also fosters skill development. Children are most interested in what they are presently doing, more than what they did before or may do later. They are particularly receptive to the therapist's descriptions of their ongoing activities. The salience of the therapist's words can be used to advantage in fostering skill development. The therapist focuses his or her descriptions on those skills and themes most relevant to the child's presenting problems. For example, for a child with social skills deficits, the therapist might focus descriptions on sharing: "The queen likes the king because the king shared his candy." For a young child who presents with a history of cruelty to animals, the therapist might look for opportunities to describe nurturing (e.g., "Your monkey is taking good care of its baby.")

Finally, descriptive statements can increase a child's awareness and acceptance of feelings that contribute to negative behavior. By attending to and describing the range of emotions children express as they play, the therapist begins the process of helping children identify their feelings and link them with their behavior (e.g., "Talking about your mother makes you feel sad.") When children see that their feelings are noticed and accepted, they become more likely to accept their feelings as well. This is a necessary step in the learning process for children who must incorporate new, more acceptable coping behaviors.

Selective Use of Description. In short-term play therapy, only those behaviors that contribute to therapy productivity are described. Obviously, it is counterproductive to reward negative attention-seeking behaviors (e.g., sticking one's tongue out at the therapist) by describing them. It is also not productive to describe neutral behaviors that distract the therapist and child from accomplishing session objectives. Suppose that a child is given a task to generate a list of positive self-statements. If the child begins to make each letter using a different color of marker, it would impede progress toward the session objective to encourage this behavior with descriptions. Even though this behavior could not be categorized as disruptive, it consumes valuable therapy time and thus would not be described.

Descriptions should be directed to the particular goals of the therapy session. Early in treatment, descriptions serve the function of establishing rapport. An initial, simple description of the child's activity can be the surest way to communicate a genuine message of acceptance. Later in therapy, descriptions with the greatest therapeutic value are those tailored to the specific treatment goals. A single activity can be described in different ways. For example, when drawing with a child who places an X through the picture, the therapist first determines whether to describe this at all. Then the therapist offers a description that strategically emphasizes a particular aspect of the behavior. In the example above, the descriptive statement, "You're crossing her totally out" would have a different impact than the statement, "Now you're finished with this picture."

Developmental Issues. Descriptive statements must always be directed to the child's age and developmental level. The therapist's descriptions must be carefully chosen so that the younger child understands the comment, and the older child does not interpret the statement as condescending. For example, the description, "Your new earrings look so grown-up!" might help to establish rapport with a six-year-old, but might have a negative effect with a 10-year-old. The amount of information contained in each descriptive statement must also be varied for children of different ages. With preschool children, the descriptions should be short sentences that contain single, concrete ideas. Although older children can understand more complex descriptions, it is sometimes helpful to check their understanding.

Reflection

Definition and Examples. Reflective statements repeat or paraphrase the child's statements. They may contain the same words used by the child or synonymous words or phrases. Therapists may choose to reflect only a part of the child's statement or may choose to elaborate upon it. The key feature of a reflection is that it does not change the basic meaning of the child's statement. Examples of reflective statements include the following:

Child: *"This is the big piece."*
Therapist: *"That is a big piece."*

Child: *"He's cool to let us go early."*
Therapist: *"You like him for not making you wait."*

Child: *"I was home by myself and I heard a loud noise and I put the covers over my head."*
Therapist: *"You were home by yourself and you felt scared."*

Child: *"My uncle unzipped my pants and kissed me down there."*
Therapist: *"Your uncle kissed you down there."*

Child: *"When I met my new foster mom, I felt like there were birds in my stomach."*
Therapist: *"Sounds like you were feeling nervous about meeting her."*

Rationale. Reflective statements increase the child's verbal communication. Children are likely to talk more to the therapist when their statements are reflected because they feel they are really being understood. Reflections also allow the child to agree or disagree with the therapist's understanding and to elaborate with further detail.

Reflective statements also can build self confidence. More than any other process skill in child therapy, reflection conveys to children the therapist's understanding and acceptance of their thoughts and ideas. The uncritical acceptance of their words gives children confidence in their ideas and reinforces their expression in therapy. Therapists will have the opportunity at times to reflect not only the child's words, but also the feelings behind the words. The reflection of feelings lets the child know that emotional expression is permissible and that it is safe to share feelings in play therapy.

Selective Use of Reflection. Selective reflection is another technique that play therapists can use to guide the content of talk toward the most salient issues. Most statements that children make contain at least two potential topics that can be pursued. Suppose that a child in therapy said, "I get mad when he takes my stuff, but mom makes him give it back." The therapist has many options in choosing what to reflect. A reflection such as, "When your brother takes your stuff it makes you really angry," is likely to elicit further comment on the child's angry feelings. On the other hand, the reflection, "Your mom will help you out," is likely to lead the conversation to comments about the child's mother.

Selective reflection can also be used to discourage children from bringing up tangential and irrelevant information. Children generally prefer to talk about movies and skateboarding rather than feelings and problems. If children are not redirected, much therapy time is lost while the therapist attends to lengthy stories about extraneous topics. The following is an example of how selective use of reflection can encourage a child to stay on topic:

> **Therapist:** *"Your mom told me that she got a phone call from your principal today because of a problem on the playground. Tell me what happened."*
>
> **Child:** [shrugs shoulders] *"We were playing basketball and somebody got hurt. Oh! Did you see the Suns' game last night? They were awesome. The score wasn't even close. My dad and I are going to get to go see a game for my birthday. I hope I get in-line skates this year."*
>
> **Therapist:** *"So, somebody got hurt while you were playing basketball on the playground."*

Developmental Issues. With preschool-age children, it is preferable to use reflections that incorporate the child's exact words. This strategy allows the therapist to talk with these children at their own developmental level using words they clearly understand. For older children, the content of reflection must be paraphrased and elaborated so as not to seem mocking or condescending.

Praise

Definition and Examples. Praise is a statement that expresses approval of the child's activities, qualities, or products. Because children tend to repeat behaviors that elicit therapist attention and approval, praise can be used to encourage children's productivity in therapy. We distinguish between two types of praise: unlabeled and labeled. Unlabeled praise is a general comment indicating approval such as: "Fantastic!," "Radical!," "Good work," "Thank you very much," and "Super!" In contrast, labeled praise is one that tells the child exactly what he or she did that the therapist liked. Examples of the use of labeled praise in play therapy include:

> *"I like how you are paying such close attention when I talk."*
> *"You're doing a good job of talking about your feelings today."*
> *"Wow! You really tried hard on that one. Give me a high five."*
> *"That's very nice of you to clean up the toys."*
> *"Thanks for waiting so patiently while I've been talking to your mom."*
> *"You're taking very good care of the toys today."*
> *"Super job of remembering the playroom rules."*

The term "praise," as described above, encompasses what others have referred to as "encouragement" (e.g., Dinkmeyer & McKay, 1983). We praise not only children's accomplishments, but their effort, improvement, and attentiveness.

Rationale. Praise is an important tool for building rapport and helping young children to feel safe and accepted by the therapist. When children are praised, their confidence in their own abilities is raised. They are more likely to take risks in therapy and attempt difficult tasks. Praise is particularly helpful for young children with low self-esteem. Additionally, labeled praise is an effective strategy for managing disruptive behavior that interferes with therapy progress (see Chapter Four). In traditional play therapy approaches, praise is typically avoided. According to Axline (1947):

> Encouragement, approval, and praise are taboo in a non-directive play-therapy session. Such reactions on the part of the therapist have a tendency either to influence the type of activities or to foster feelings of guilt. The same is true of disapproval or negative criticism. The atmosphere must be neutral. (p. 97)

We agree that praise influences the way children behave during play therapy and does not allow them to fully lead the play. In a short-term approach, however, it is essential that we influence children's behavior so that work can be accomplished in an expedient fashion. Therapists may also be reluctant to use praise because of the concern that children will only share thoughts and feelings that they think will lead to therapist approval. For that reason, we are careful to praise children for the process of expressing thoughts and feelings, whatever they might be. From the first session of therapy, children are given labeled praise for using "I feel..." statements for both positive and negative feelings, being honest about misbehavior, talking about things that are hard, and admitting mistakes.

Another reason some therapists are hesitant to use praise is because it communicates a value judgement. Therapists are concerned that children's self-esteem may become too dependent on what others, particularly the therapist, think of them. Additionally, there is a concern that children with disruptive behavior who have low self-esteem will reject the praise because it is dissonant with their negative self-image. As an alternative to praise, other authors have recommended that therapists simply acknowledge children's accomplishments and attributes. For example, Berne and Savary (1990) suggest the following:

> Recognize what is positive and successful in a child's work or behavior, then acknowledge it by describing what you see and how you feel. Whenever possible, avoid evaluating children, their behavior, or what they do, even if your evaluation is favorable. (p. 50)

We believe that praise is important, particularly for children who have low self-esteem, though we recognize that some children will initially reject the praise. According to Crary (1993), children are more likely to reject unlabeled than labeled praise:

> General praise often contributes to a feeling of well-being and competence, but it can backfire if the child himself does not feel 'good' or 'nice' at the moment. When that happens the child may do something to show the parent that he or she is not nice or good after all. This would have been avoided if the parent had said what he saw or what she felt about the situation, because what was being praised would be clear. (p. 59)

Children with low self-esteem may also reject labeled praise that is provided sincerely. They may become anxious and interrupt the therapist, or they may say something like, "Don't say that." We still believe that labeled praise serves an important function. Even though the child does not believe the praise at that moment, the words were heard. If they are told often enough, in enough situations, and by enough people, each instance praise will have a cumulative impact, chipping away at a child's low self-esteem.

Developmental Issues. For children age 7 and younger, we recommend that therapists use labeled praise at a very high frequency. Over a 50-minute therapy session, we typically praise approximately 25 times, which averages out to one praise every two minutes. With older children, however, this rate of praise would be excessive. Developmentally, children over the age of seven are more socially aware. When praised, they are likely to evaluate their own performance against their perceptions of the abilities of peers. If they do not perceive themselves as worthy of the praise or determine that the therapist's praise is not genuine, they will reject it and rapport may be weakened. Thus, we recommend that therapists use praise less frequently with older children and that the statements be carefully selected and sincerely delivered.

Questions

Definition and Examples. A question makes an explicit demand upon the child to provide specific information and, when used in moderation, is helpful in guiding children to talk about areas of concern. Questions are often anxiety-arousing to children in the beginning sessions of therapy, but tend to become more productive with time. Examples of questions that might be asked in play therapy include the following:

> *"When does your daddy come visit you?"*
> *"What chores does your mother want you to do?"*
> *"Where could you put it so it will be safe?"*
> *"Who do you want to go with you?"*
> *"Which one of my cards shows how you feel when your dad yells at you?"*
> *"Looking back on it now, what would you do differently?"*

Rationale. A question is one of the most direct ways of soliciting specific information for further use in therapy. Open-ended questions (those that begin with "wh. . . ") are usually more fruitful than closed-ended questions (which can be answered "yes" or "no") because they elicit more thoughtful information. To illustrate, the question, "Do you like to visit your dad?" could get a "no" answer. Several follow-up questions might be needed to elicit the child's thoughts and feelings about such a visit, consuming more time than is preferable in a short-term therapy. In contrast, "How do you feel about visiting your dad?" is more likely to elicit a thoughtful response. Open-ended questions also greatly decrease the chance that the therapist will inadvertently lead the child to state conclusions that are suggested by the question itself. For example, a leading question such as, "Do you think you need to tell her you'll pay for it?" will likely get a "yes" answer, but is less likely to lead to meaningful problem-solving than an open-ended question like, "What do you think you need to do?"

There are a few situations in child therapy, however, when a closed-ended question is helpful for pinning down a specific fact. For example, a child who has been abused may have been instructed not to talk about abusive incidents. With a hesitant child, a therapist might want to ask a closed-ended question such as, "Have you been told not to talk to me about that?" permitting a short, less threatening answer.

One type of question that is generally counterproductive in play therapy is one that begins with "why." A "why" question is almost universally perceived by children as an accusation, requiring them to justify their behavior rather than to describe it. In addition to placing the child on the defensive, a "why" question may lead to hostile feelings toward the therapist. For example, a question such as, "Why didn't you tell her what you did?" would be better rephrased, "What did you think might happen if you told her?" Kanfer, Eyberg, and Krahn (1992) discourage the use of "why" questions, explaining that "it is the interviewer's responsibility to determine motivation; it is unproductive to ask the child to make these interpretations (pg. 53)."

Selective Use of Questions. Like many adults, therapists tend to overuse questions, particularly with young children. Questions are used in an attempt to stimulate children to talk. Questions are only effective, however, if therapists use them sparingly and pause to provide children with opportunities to respond. Recognizing that most children are interested in answering only a limited number of questions each session, we recommend reserving questions for key moments. Therefore we would avoid unproductive exchanges such as the following:

Therapist: *"What are you coloring? Is that a snowman?"*
Child: [does not respond]
Therapist: *"Are those his eyes? He is smiling, isn't he? Have you made snowmen at your house?"*
Child: *"Uh-huh."*

By reducing the overall number of questions, the child's response rate is significantly improved. Thus, the odds of getting a thoughtful response to a meaningful question are greatly increased.

Interpretation

Definition and Examples. An interpretation is a statement that makes a link between a child's behavior and his or her motivations or feelings. The interpretation is made to bring the link to the child's attention or awareness. Whereas descriptions comment on a straightforward aspect of the child's demeanor or behavior, interpretations involve a greater level of inference. An interpretation is an educated "best guess" as to the beliefs or feelings that may be motivating the child's behavior. Because it is an hypothesis, an interpretation is always stated tentatively so that the child can agree or disagree. Interpretations commonly are stated with tentative beginnings, such as "I wonder," "Maybe," or "Sometimes." Examples of interpretation include the following:

Child: *"I hate my stupid sister and her stupid wheelchair."*
Therapist: *"Maybe you're feeling angry at her today because she gets so much of your parents' attention."*
Child: [has a history of social withdrawal] *"None of the guys want to play with me because I don't have a basketball hoop."*
Therapist: *"You're feeling sad because you don't have many friends. Perhaps the reason*

> *they aren't coming over to play is that you haven't asked them lately."*
>
> **Therapist:** *"I don't see your stepfather in your family drawing. What can you tell me about that?"*
>
> **Child:** *"Can I go show this to my mom?"*
>
> **Therapist:** *"I wonder if you want to avoid talking to me about your stepfather."*
>
> **Child:** *"Should I put the red one here?"*
>
> **Therapist:** *"It seems like every time you want to put a block on you ask me if it's okay. Maybe you are afraid that I won't like you if you don't make the best choice."*

Because interpretation is an inference, it is possible to "misinterpret" or to interpret a feeling that the child is not ready to acknowledge. If a child disagrees with an interpretation, it is best to accept what the child says and let it go. There will be other opportunities to help the child work through difficult material.

Rationale. Disruptive children often use misbehavior rather than words to express negative emotions. Upon entering therapy, they may not have a vocabulary for expressing feelings and may be unaware of the relationships between thoughts, feelings, and behaviors. Interpretations are a helpful way of teaching children about these relationships, paving the way for verbal expression of affect and self-control of behavior. Additionally, interpretations help children to gain insight into behavioral patterns. This process stimulates children to view issues and problems from a different perspective, facilitating conflict resolution. Consider the above example of a withdrawn child who believed that he had few friends because he did not have a basketball hoop. Through the therapist's interpretation, the child was given an opportunity to consider that a lack of assertiveness could be contributing to the child's social isolation.

Selective Use of Interpretation. In traditional play therapy, disruptive behavior is viewed as rich clinical material often requiring immediate interpretation. As discussed in Chapter One, however, the traditional process of working through disruptive behavior cannot be accomplished within the time constraints of a short-term therapy. Therefore, our play therapy approach is designed to minimize behavior problems. From a behavioral perspective, immediate interpretations give children rewarding attention for disruptive behaviors, thereby increasing their rate of occurrence. We believe that the majority of disruptive behavior displayed by children in therapy is extraneous "noise" and is performed either to achieve stimulating negative attention or to avoid unattractive tasks. We recognize, however, that children sometimes act out in response to sensitive and conflictual material being addressed in therapy. In our play therapy approach, we attempt to provide interpretations only for disruptive behavior that occurs in response to conflictual material. Thus, it is important to evaluate the cause (or function) of the misbehavior.

To determine why a child is acting out, it is helpful to examine the antecedents to the misbehavior. Suppose that a child throws a toy at the observation mirror. If this had occurred subsequent to a therapist direction to clean up the toys, it probably served the function of task avoidance. If the throwing had occurred after a statement from the child such as, "Watch me hit your reflection in the mirror," we might assume that the behavior was designed to elicit negative attention from the therapist. In contrast, the throwing might have occurred after the therapist confronted the child's fantasies regarding the reconciliation of his divorcing parents. In this case, the disruptive behavior likely served as a means of expressing anger and helplessness. We would not offer an interpretation when throwing occurs as a function of task avoidance or attention-seeking. Instead, we would use one of the behavior management strategies described in Chapter Four. We would, however, offer an interpretation when throwing serves to express negative feelings that are directly relevant to the content of therapy.

We offer immediate interpretations when children are behaving appropriately. Immediate interpretations are advantageous because children are most receptive to input given in the context of a "teachable moment." When children are engaging in misbehavior, however, delayed interpretations are preferred. By delaying the feedback, children may be given the same information without immediately rewarding misbehavior with therapist attention. An additional benefit of delayed feedback is that children may not be able to assimilate an interpretation when engaging in uncontrolled disruptive behavior (e.g., screaming, throwing a temper tantrum). Interpretation may be more effective if provided later, when the child has calmed down.

Before resorting to delayed interpretation, we prompt children by saying something like, "Please use your words instead of your behavior to tell me how you are feeling." If the child responds by using words or discontinuing disruptive behavior, the therapist may offer an immediate interpretation (e.g., "I notice you're smiling when you talk about school. I wonder if you feel proud of yourself when you earn the points.") If the child continues the misbehavior, an interpretation will be provided at a later time, after the behavior has been effectively managed (see Chapter Four).

Delayed interpretations may be either direct (i.e., explicitly addressing the child's behavior or feelings) or metaphorical (i.e., symbolically addressing the child's behavior or feelings through puppets, dolls, etc.) An example of a delayed, but direct, interpretation is as follows:

Therapist: *"Now we are going to pretend like this is the courtroom so you can practice how you talk in court."*

Child: [hides under table and whines] *"Shut up! I don't want to!"*

Therapist: [prompts] *"Please use your feeling words like we practiced earlier."*

Child: [stays under table and begins kicking feet and crying]

Therapist: [ignores and distracts] *"I think I'll get out my special markers and see how many colors I can put in a rainbow. Here's a pretty pink color."*

Child: [comes out from under the table a few minutes later] *"Put some blue clouds in the sky."*

Therapist: [returns attention] *"Thanks for coming out from under the table. Sure, we can put some blue clouds in the sky."*

Child: [draws with therapist]

Therapist: [after approximately one minute of calm play, provides an interpretation] *"When you hid under the table a couple of minutes ago, I wonder if you were feeling scared about going to court."*

Child: *"I hate court. I don't want to talk about that."*

Therapist: *"I like how you just used your words instead of your behavior to show me your feelings. Court can be a scary thing. I know some ways to make kids not feel so scared when they go to court. One of them is pretty fun. We can make a pretend courtroom right here in our playroom! You're going to get a chance to earn stickers for helping me out."*

A delayed interpretation may also be offered in the form of a metaphor in which a fantasy character performs the behavior, or discusses the behavior with another fantasy character. For example, the therapist could note that, "The little girl puppet is hiding under the table because she is scared about going to court. She has forgotten to use her words to show her feelings. She will feel a lot less scared if she talks about it. Here is a puppet for you. Would you like to help the little girl use her feeling words?" Children may be less defensive about accepting interpretations that are made metaphorically because the threatening feelings are processed indirectly.

Imitation

Definition and Examples. At its simplest, imitation is doing what the child is doing in a way that does not interfere with the child's play. One form of imitation involves parallel play. The therapist engages in the same activity as the child, but plays separately (e.g., the therapist builds a tower beside the tower the child is building). Imitation also can involve cooperative play in which similar actions contribute to a common game (e.g., adding blocks to the child's tower according to the child's plan). To imitate successfully, the therapist stays a step behind the child in the task and watches the child's reactions carefully to be sure that the play is acceptable.

Rationale. Imitation is a strategy for allowing children to lead the play, while building self-esteem and strengthening the therapeutic alliance. By imitating the child's play, the therapist conveys a message that the child is engaged in an acceptable and desirable activity. Imitating also increases children's imitation of the therapist. Children usually feel good about the therapist entering into their game, and they will often respond by imitating the therapist in return. Imitation also promotes basic social interaction skills such as turn-taking and sharing (see Chapter Seven).

Selective Use of Imitation. Children in play vacillate among levels of maturity as they alternate between their desire for the safety of what is familiar and their striving to try new things and to learn. The play therapist may imitate all of these levels of play as long as the behavior does not interfere with therapy productivity. Because children have a tendency to imitate the therapist, therapists should avoid modeling behaviors that are unacceptable if displayed by the child (e.g., leaving the room to retrieve new materials, sitting on the table, playing aggressively with the toys).

Developmental Issues. Imitation is a helpful technique for engaging children at their level of cognitive and social development. The nature of the imitation must be adapted when working with children of different ages. Children younger than six enjoy having the therapist mirror their activities exactly. It may be a relief to them to play with an adult who reinforces their competence without pushing them beyond their zone of proximal development. Young children feel special and capable when therapists imitate their play precisely (e.g., child scribbles with a yellow crayon, and therapist duplicates the scribble with his or her own crayon). Older children enjoy imitation which takes the form of more interactive and elaborative play. They respond best to more subtle imitation in which the therapist engages in a similar activity without copying their exact play (e.g., child builds a rocket, and therapist builds a launching pad). The therapist must be careful to avoid playing at a more accomplished level than that of the child. If the therapist "imitates" the child's drawing by sketching a landscape with shading and perspective, the child is likely to feel inadequate and to become disinterested in the activity.

4

STRATEGIES FOR MANAGING DISRUPTIVE BEHAVIOR

In previous chapters we have discussed features of our short-term play therapy approach which inhibit disruptive behavior. For example, the structure of sessions emphasizes pre-established rules, consistent routines for transitions, careful attention to precedents, choosing appealing Child's Work activities, and requiring work before play. Yet, even with these preventive features in place, disruptive children can become resistant, overstimulated, or off-task, particularly during therapist-directed activities. This chapter presents a number of strategies for managing disruptive behavior during play therapy including praise, tangible reinforcers, rules for being a good listener, contingent attention, effective directions, the "When-Then" strategy, special game rules, the "Turtle Technique" of self-control, and physical guidance for dangerous behaviors.

Praise

Praise is one of the most powerful behavior management strategies available to play therapists. Most children, even those with disruptive behavior disorders, will alter their behavior to earn the approval of adults. As mentioned in Chapter Three, praise may be classified as either "unlabeled" or "labeled." Unlabeled praise is a general comment indicating approval, while labeled praise is that which tells the child exactly what he or she did that the therapist liked (e.g., "Great job of sitting still while we read the book.").

For behavior management purposes, labeled praise is generally more effective than unlabeled praise because it informs the child about the specific behaviors that are required to attain additional approval. A child who receives a specific praise for helping the therapist clean up the toys is likely to want to help in the future in order to receive more praise. However, a child who receives an unlabeled praise such as "great" when making a list of feeling words may not understand what the therapist is pleased about. In this instance, the unlabeled praise could refer to penmanship, cooperation with the task, spelling, effort, creativity, length of the list, etc. While unlabeled praise helps children to feel good about themselves and their activities, it is often too vague to result in behavioral improvement.

Using labeled praise to modify disruptive behavior is a three-step process. First, the therapist identifies a problematic behavior that could interfere with therapeutic productivity, such as running around the room. Second, the therapist identifies one or more behaviors that are incompatible with or opposite the problematic behavior. In the case of running around the room, incompatible behaviors would include sitting still, walking, and working on a puzzle. The third step is to construct one or more examples of labeled praise that can be used to reward the child for incompatible behavior. Therapists can prevent disruptive behavior by using these steps proactively to "catch the child being good." For a child with a history of trying to run out of the playroom, the therapist should look for the first opportunity upon entering the playroom to offer praise such as, "Good job of remembering the rule about staying in the playroom." See Table 4-1 for more examples of how to use labeled praise to encourage cooperation during play therapy.

Occasionally, an oppositional child may respond to labeled praise by engaging in misbehavior. Consider the following example of a defiant four-year-old:

> **Child:** [screams] *"Look! My plane crashed."*
> **Therapist:** [ignores and models the opposite behavior] *"I'm a good pilot. I'm going to fly my plane carefully and land safely."*
> **Child:** [plays gently] *"I'm going to put gas in my plane."*
> **Therapist:** [offers labeled praise] *"I like it when you play gently with the plane."*
> **Child:** [smiles mischievously and crashes plane into therapist's plane] *"Dogfight!"*

Following the therapist's praise, the child's behavior immediately worsened instead of improving as expected. It would be easy to erroneously assume that praise is not effective with this child. There is an alternative explanation, however, that could account for this reaction. Many times, children will react oppositionally to labeled praise in order to obtain very stimulating negative attention. In such situations, it is best to ignore the negative attention-seeking behavior rather than to interpret it. When children perceive that their misbehavior did not have the desired effect (i.e., gaining stimulating negative attention), they typically try to regain the therapist's attention using positive behavior. To illustrate, the following is a continuation of the previous example:

> **Child:** [smiles mischievously and crashes plane into therapist's plane] *"Dogfight!"*
> **Therapist:** [turns partially away and plays alone] *"I'm playing very gently with my plane."*
> **Child:** [says urgently] *"I'm playing gently now, too!"*
> **Therapist:** [returns attention] *"Oh, it's so much more fun to play with you when you play gently with the plane."*

Tangible and Edible Reinforcers

With only 12 sessions to effect change, it is important to find expedient ways to modify children's behavior. In short-term play therapy, children are challenged to accomplish a great deal of work in a short amount of time. Although therapists always try to make Child's Work activities intrinsically interesting, there are times when important activities may not be appealing to the child. For example, confronting one's fears through systematic desensitization is not pleasurable for children, nor is overpracticing a social skill. When working with disruptive children, resistance to nonpreferred activities is particularly strong and problematic. Tangible and edible reinforcers are powerful and efficient tools for motivating disruptive children to cooperate. Rewards can serve as positive and viable alternatives to power struggles and confrontive management strategies.

There are unlimited possibilities for the design of in-session reward programs. The best systems provide immediate rewards for well-defined and specific behaviors. A system that does not meet these guidelines would be one in which a child receives a treat if he or she is "good" all session. This program is likely to fail because the behavioral expectations are too

Table 4-1. Using Labeled Praise to Encourage Cooperation During Play Therapy

Problem Behavior	Opposite/Incompatible Behavior	Labeled Praise
Leaving the room	Staying in the room	Thank you for staying in the room.
Throwing toys	Keeping the toys on the table	Good job keeping your toys on the table.
Running around	Walking	I like it when you walk inside.
Hiding from the therapist	Being where the therapist can see him/her	I'm glad that you're sitting where I can see you.
Playing roughly with toys	Playing gently with the toys	You're taking nice care of my toys.
Touching off-limits materials	Keeping hands to oneself	Terrific job keeping your hands to yourself.
Yelling	Using an indoor voice	You're using your nice, quiet indoor voice.
Putting feet on the table	Putting feet on the floor	I appreciate your keeping your feet on the floor.
Doing cartwheels indoors	Playing calmly	It's fun to play with you when you play calmly.
Whining	Using a big boy or girl voice	I can understand you very well when you use your big boy voice.
Bossiness	Asking nicely	What polite manners!
Difficulty waiting for turn	Taking turns	It's very nice of you to take turns.
Gazing out the window	Paying attention	You're really being a good listener right now.
Coloring on the table	Coloring on the paper	You are being very careful to mark only on the paper.
Refusing to comply	Following instructions	Super job following instructions.
Running ahead during transitions	Walking alongside the therapist	Thanks for staying right with me.
Ignoring the therapist's questions	Answering questions	I like it when you answer my questions.
Giving silly responses	Giving serious answers	It's good that you thought really hard about that answer.
Climbing on furniture	Sitting on furniture	Good remembering to sit still on my couch.

high and vague, and the reward is too delayed. Greater success could be expected by simply using a hand stamp or sticker as an immediate reward for exhibiting a specific desirable behavior (e.g., good listening). In general, hand stamps are preferred over stickers because children can manipulate stickers (e.g., repeatedly change their placement) and become distracted. If stickers are to be used, it may be advisable to use a sticker book or chart. In this system, the child still receives the immediate reward of the sticker. Distractions are minimized, however, because the therapist can keep the sticker book/chart until the "termination party" on the last day of treatment.

A variation of the sticker chart may be used to combine both immediate and delayed rewards. Many disruptive children, particularly those over the age of five, respond favorably to a program in which they earn points over multiple sessions and later receive a prize for accumulated points. Points may be earned for demonstrating good listening skills, cooperating with a work assignment, cleaning up toys, and using words to communicate feelings. Over the course of a session, therapists can keep track of points by marking them on a chalkboard or piece of paper. Immediately following the clean up of Child's Play toys, points are exchanged for stickers which the child places on a recording chart. The chart is a graphic representation of the child's progress toward earning a reward (see Appendix for a sample chart). In this system, the child earns three types of rewards: (a) immediate (points), (b) slightly delayed (getting to put stickers on chart), and (c) delayed (tangible/edible rewards). Because the tangible/edible rewards are given infrequently over the course of treatment (e.g., every three sessions), expenses are kept to a minimum, and the rewards remain novel. Examples of rewards that can be provided when the child has progressed to the end of the chart include: selecting a small toy from a treasure chest, getting to play basketball with the therapist, receiving a ribbon/certificate, and making popcorn with the therapist.

Rules for Being a Good Listener

One of the greatest challenges in doing play therapy with disruptive children is maintaining their attention. In each session, there are many times when a child's undivided attention is required. Examples include: (a) when the therapist is explaining directions for role-play; (b) when a therapeutic book is being read to the child; (c) when a key interpretation is about to be offered; and (d) when children are asked to rehearse skills for parents. Disruptive children often respond to therapist attempts to gain their attention by looking the other way, fidgeting, and interrupting with irrelevant verbalizations. Thus, in our short-term therapy approach, children are taught in the first few sessions how to be good listeners.

Children are taught the three "good listening rules:" (1) Look right in my eyes when I talk; (2) Hold your body very, very still; and (3) Think hard about what I am saying (McGinnis & Goldstein, 1990a; 1990b). During sessions, children are asked to practice good listening and are given praise and a sticker or hand stamp for demonstrating the skills. When the therapist needs to elicit the child's attention, a prompt can be given such as, "Show me your good listening skills." Children are rewarded for responding to the prompt as well as for spontaneous use of good listening skills.

Strategic Ignoring and Contingent Attention

As mentioned in Chapter One, contingent attention is arguably the most powerful strategy available for dealing with disruptive behavior. Its power stems from the fact that negative attention-seeking is a primary function of such misbehaviors as yelling, running around the room, hiding from the therapist, and rambunctious play. By strategically ignoring negative attention-seeking behaviors and selectively attending to desirable behaviors, the therapist can enhance child productivity in play therapy. Strategic ignoring involves breaking eye contact and orienting the therapist's body away from the child. It is important that ignoring not be subtle so that children may be quickly motivated to re-earn the therapist's attention. Out of respect and fairness to children, strategic ignoring is explained and modeled in advance. Children are taught which misbehaviors will be ignored and which positive behaviors will allow the therapist to interact with the child again. By explaining the skill of ignoring in advance, the behavioral escalation that commonly accompanies the withdrawal of attention can be prevented or minimized. Strategic ignoring is explained to children in the following way:

> Sometimes during our play time you may see me turn around like this and play by myself (therapist models withdrawing attention). This is called ignoring. I use ignoring when children play roughly, act bossy, make guns or swords with the toys, or forget to use their indoor voice. But as soon as children remember to play gently and nicely, I turn back around to play with them again right away (therapist models returning the attention).

Ignoring/Modeling. Strategic ignoring is most efficient when it is supplemented with a strategy that promotes positive alternative behaviors. One such strategy is to model an opposite, incompatible behavior. When a child displays a negative attention-seeking behavior such as aggressive play with zoo animals, the therapist can turn away and model nurturing behavior with the animals (e.g., petting and feeding the zebra). While modeling, the therapist can describe with animation how the animal is being cared for and how much the animal appreciates being treated nicely. Any verbalizations by the therapist during ignoring are restricted to descriptions of therapist activity and are not said directly to the child. Children typically respond to this ignoring/modeling strategy by discontinuing problematic behavior and imitating or showing interest in the therapist's prosocial behavior. As soon as the child engages in a positive or nondisruptive behavior (e.g., feeds the donkey), the therapist returns the attention by offering enthusiastic labeled praise (e.g., "You are taking good care of the donkey now. He likes that.").

Ignoring/Distracting. When ignoring a disruptive behavior, an opposite or incompatible behavior may not be immediately apparent and therefore cannot be modeled. In such cases, the therapist may choose to make ignoring more efficient by pairing it with distraction. The purpose of distraction is to redirect the child away from disruptive behavior and toward any other neutral or positive behavior. The keys to successful distraction are to (a) select a stimulating activity, and (b) describe the activity with exaggerated enthusiasm. The goal of ignoring/distracting is to motivate the child to discontinue the problem behavior by withdrawing all attention while making another activity appear highly attractive. The following example illustrates the combined use of ignoring and distraction:

Child: [dives under table and giggles] *"You can't find me!"*
Therapist: [ignores and distracts] *"I'm going to see what is in this bucket [shakes bucket]. Oh, it's my favorite toy! It's Mrs. Potato Head! I'm going to put a*

moustache on her. She looks silly!"
Child: [peeks out from under table] *"She's a girl. Girl's don't have moustaches."*
Therapist: [continues ignoring because child is still under table] *"Poor Mrs. Potato Head can't see. I need to figure out how to help her to see."*
Child: [scrambles out from under the table] *"I know how. She needs some eyes."*
Therapist: *"Oh, what a great idea! I'm glad that you came out from under the table so I can play with you again."*

Whether using distraction or modeling, it is important that the therapist remember to ignore the child entirely until a desired behavior is demonstrated. In particular, therapists should avoid making remarks to the child like, "I wish I had somebody to play with," "Boy, it's lonely over here," "The puppy wants a little girl to come and take him for a walk," and "Mr. Potato Head wants to know where Michael is." Remarks like this provide indirect attention to the child and often prolong misbehavior.

Giving Good Directions

Because a great deal of therapy work must be accomplished in a short period of time, it is important for the therapist to be effective in eliciting compliance. The way instructions are stated plays a major role in children's responsivity to therapist-directed interactions. An important distinction can be made between "suggestions" and "directions." In our short-term play therapy, suggestions are defined as leading questions intended to guide the child in a particular direction. Examples of suggestions include the following: "Would you like to draw a picture of your family now?" "How about sitting in the chair next to me?" "Could you be a big helper and pick up these blocks for me?" In contrast, directions are defined as specific instructions that the child is told to follow. Directions are provided as statements, not questions. Examples of directions include the following: "Please draw a picture of your family," "Sit in this chair next to me," and "Please pick up the blocks."

We find both suggestions and directions to be useful tools, but their effectiveness depends on the context and purpose of the instructions. Because suggestions are phrased in a way that communicates that the child has a choice, we reserve our use of suggestions for times when we are truly comfortable with whatever the child decides. For example, to a child who is in foster care and has written a story about his biological mother, we might say: "I'm really glad you talked about those feelings. Would you like to share your story with your mother?" In this situation, it is therapeutic and appropriate for the child to decide whether or not to follow this suggestion. Along these lines, it may be appropriate to suggest that a particular toy be brought to the Check-Out room to entertain the child during adult conversation. A suggestion is a good strategy in this case because the child should have some choice about preferred toys.

Whereas suggestions are good therapeutic tools in that they allow children to maintain some control, they are less effective than directions when it comes to behavior management and eliciting cooperation with therapist-directed activities. Both clinicians and researchers in the area of disruptive behavior disorders have discovered that acting-out children are more likely to comply with directions than suggestions (e.g., Hembree-Kigin & McNeil, 1995). Knowing this, we use directions rather than suggestions in situations in which it is important that children comply. For example, directions would be used when children begin to run ahead during transition times (e.g., "Please come back and walk with me."); when specific activities need to be completed during Child's Work (e.g., "Please pick the card that shows how you felt when you visited your mother."); when overstimulated children need to be calmed down (e.g., "Show me your breathing exercises."); and when distractible children need to be brought back to task (e.g., "Show me you are being a good listener.") When choosing to use a direction, the child is more likely to cooperate if the direction is stated with a definitive and confident tone of voice. Other factors that will increase the effectiveness of directions are detailed in Table 4-2.

The "When-Then" Strategy

The "When-Then" strategy is most commonly used when a child has failed to comply with a direction, is dawdling, or has begun a minor disruptive behavior. Children are told that a pleasant, rewarding activity will be provided once they engage in a specified behavior. The therapist states the contingency by saying something like, "When you practice how to handle teasing one more time, then we can use our colored chalk on the chalkboard." To make this strategy work, the therapist must be careful to make the consequence more rewarding than what the child is already doing. As there is much variation in the degree of reinforcement that children will derive from various activities and tangible rewards, the therapist must tailor the consequences to fit the individual child. Suppose the therapist wants to switch to the new Child's Work activity of reading a book about a parent who is terminally ill, but the child wants to continue coloring a picture of the hospital. If the consequence of reading the book is not very rewarding for this particular child, it probably would be ineffective for the therapist to say, "When you come sit next to me, then we can begin reading." If, however, the situation permitted the therapist to switch to an activity that this particular child found rewarding (perhaps playing a therapeutic game), the When-Then strategy probably would be effective. For those situations which involve a transition to a less rewarding activity, a tangible reinforcer can be incorporated into the When-Then strategy (e.g., "When you sit next to me, then I will put a sticker in your sticker book."). See Table 4-3 for additional examples of commonly used When-Then statements during play therapy.

Special Game Rules

"Special game rules" is an excellent strategy for gaining the cooperation of resistant children. Some of the reasons that children may be resistant to therapist-directed activities include: (a) boredom and/or frustration with the task; (b) desire to engage in a preferred activity; and (c) avoidance of anxiety-evoking material. The tool of special game rules is based on the principle that children will expend greater effort when trying to earn a turn at a fun activity. The therapist assigns special rules to games such as checkers (or other nontherapeutic board games), cards, jacks, and marbles. Typically, the special rule is that the child must produce a small unit of work in exchange for the privilege of taking a turn in the game. For example, the following special game rule might be used while playing checkers with a child who is reluctant to talk about feelings:

> Today we get to play checkers, but this is a special kind of checkers. The rule is that before we can take a turn, we each have to tell about a time that we felt an emotion. Before the first turn, we will talk about happy. On the second turn we will talk about

Table 4-2. Using Good Directions to Promote Child Cooperation

Strategy	Rationale	Examples
Give directions one at a time	Some children can't remember multiple-part directions	*Avoid:* "Pretend that the puppet is being teased, and tell me what the puppet should say, and then tell me what the outcome would be." *Better:* "Pretend that the puppet is being teased. Good work. Now, tell me what the puppet should say."
Break directions down into small parts	Avoids overwhelming child Child gets more opportunities for praise	*Avoid:* "Clean up the toys." *Better:* "Please put the lion in the box. You're a great helper. Now, put the crayons in the bucket."
State directions positively (tell child what to do, instead of what not to do)	Some oppositional children rebel against "stop" and "don't" commands Tells child what he or she can do instead Allows child to do the right thing instead of just ceasing a misbehavior	*Avoid:* "Don't run." *Better:* "Please walk." *Avoid:* "Quit kicking the wall." *Better:* "Please keep your feet on the floor."
Make directions specific, not vague	Lets child know exactly what is expected Eliminates confusion	*Avoid:* "Settle down." *Better:* "Show me how you can do the turtle."
Be polite and respectful, while still being direct	Makes interactions more pleasant Models good social skills	*Avoid:* "Would you do another role-play, please?" *Better:* "Please choose a puppet for our next role-play."
Give children choices when possible	Encourages the development of autonomy and decision-making	"You can clean up now or after you take one more turn."
Use explanations strategically	In some situations, children ask "why" because they want information. At other times, they want to delay following directions To head off arguing, explanations are best given before rather than after the direction.	*Avoid:* **Therapist:** "Please sit over here." **Child:** "Why?" **Therapist:** "Because we are going to do some work." **Child:** "Wait a minute." **Therapist:** "You can play with that later." *Better:* **Therapist:** "It's time for us to do some work now. We will have a chance to play again later. Please sit over here." **Child:** "Why?" **Therapist:** (ignores and distracts)

Adapted and reprinted by permission from Hembree-Kigin, T., & McNeil, C. B. (1995). *Parent-Child Interaction Therapy* (pp. 155-157). New York: Plenum Publishing Corporation.

sad. Then, on the third turn, we will talk about angry. And on the fourth turn, we will talk about scared. Okay, you can start. Before you move a checker, tell me about a time you felt happy. That's a good example. Now you can make your move. Now it's my turn. I can't move until I tell you about a time when I felt happy. Let's see...

Other examples of special game rules include requiring that a child use an "I statement" before drawing a card, role-play how to accept a compliment before shooting a marble, use a positive self-statement before taking a turn at jacks, and "owning up to" a mistake or misbehavior before spinning.

Table 4-3. When-Then Statements for Encouraging Cooperation in Play Therapy

When you take my hand, then I will open the door.
When you ask me nicely, then I will hand you the marker.
When you sit in the chair, then I will give you your snack.
When you use your indoor voice, then you can take a turn.
When you put the clay back in the can, then we can show this picture to your grandfather.
When you are done with your bathroom break, then we can play with some new toys.
When you show me how to relax your hands and arms, then we can take our break.
When you tell me one more story, then we can get out the paints.
When you use your words to show me you are angry, then we can play what you want to play.
When you ask me in your big girl voice, then I will answer your question.
When you play gently with the toys, then I will turn back around and play with you.

The "Turtle Technique"

A classic strategy for helping disruptive children regain self-control is the "Turtle Technique" (Robin, 1976). This technique is particularly appropriate for hyperactive children whose behavior can quickly escalate to the point of becoming rambunctious, loud, and frenetic. It is also useful in curbing negative attention-seeking behavior during conversations with parents in Check-In and Check-Out. Even children who are not hyperactive can lose self-control when presented with anxiety-evoking material. The Turtle Technique can be used to help anxious children become more calm and focused.

In this self-control technique, the therapist tells the child the story of the turtle:

Little Turtle was a handsome young turtle very upset about going to school. He always got in trouble at school because he got into fights. Other kids would tease, bump, or hit him; he would get very angry and start big fights. The teacher would have to punish him. Then one day he met the big old tortoise, who told him that his shell was the secret answer to all his problems. The tortoise told Little Turtle to withdraw into his shell when he felt angry and rest until he was no longer angry. So he tried it the next day, and it worked. The teacher now smiled at him and he no longer got into big fights. (Robin, 1976, p. 450)

Children are taught to react to aggressive impulses by imagining that they are turtles. They withdraw into their shells, pull their arms and legs close to their bodies, put their heads down, and close their eyes. The therapist can use progressive muscle relaxation to help diffuse emotional tensions. Once children are relaxed, social problem-solving strategies can be used to generate alternative responses. We prefer to introduce the Turtle Technique early in the course of treatment to assist in managing disruptive behaviors and to provide children with the opportunity to overlearn the skill by practicing it over many sessions.

Physical Guidance for Dangerous or Destructive Behavior

The overwhelming majority of disruptive behaviors can be effectively handled using techniques that involve no physical contact between the therapist and child. A more assertive strategy, however, may be required for addressing behaviors that are physically dangerous to the child or therapist or which would result in serious damage to property. Examples of these problematic behaviors include hitting the therapist, throwing chairs, self-injurious behavior, and cutting hair with scissors. In longer-term play therapy approaches, the therapist might choose to handle this type of misbehavior by ending the therapy session early and sending the child home. In a short-term play therapy approach, however, we cannot afford to lose valuable therapy time in this manner.

For dangerous or destructive behavior, we recommend that therapists use a brief restraint of the child's forearms accompanied by a succinct reminder of the playroom rules. In response to dangerous behavior, the therapist may hold the child's arms (directly above the wrists) while saying in a firm voice, "No hurting!" The therapist should then look away and continue holding the child's arms for approximately 20 seconds. At the end of the holding time, the therapist may say to the child, "I'm going to let go now. Remember our playroom rule is 'No hurting'." Then the therapist should engage in distracting and enthusiastic play to engage the child's attention. As soon as the child engages in a positive or neutral behavior, the therapist should offer labeled praise such as, "Thanks for playing in a safe way. You're doing a good job of following our playroom rules."

Given that physical restraint can weaken rapport, the incident should be processed with the child later in the session after the child has gained some affective distance. We recommend that therapists say something like this: "Do you remember when I had to hold onto your arms a little while ago? I did that because I was worried that you might get hurt. I care a lot about you, and I would never want you to be hurt. Please remember that we have to play safely in this playroom. Thanks for being a good listener." Because of the potential for physical harm when using any type of restraint, we recommend that therapists working with aggressive and/or defiant children receive training and certification in physical restraint techniques.

5

INTRODUCING FAMILIES TO PLAY THERAPY: SESSIONS ONE AND TWO

Therapy Intake Evaluation

Before beginning the first play therapy session, we always conduct a therapy intake evaluation. The purposes of this evaluation are as follows: (a) to determine whether treatment is needed and if so, which is the most appropriate intervention, (b) to collect information about presenting problems that can be used to establish treatment goals, and (c) to obtain objective data that can be used to evaluate treatment effectiveness (i.e., compare pre- and post-treatment data). Although a thorough description of the intake evaluation procedures is beyond the scope of this book, we will provide an overview of its basic components.

Parent Interview. We begin our intake evaluation with a thorough interview with the parents covering developmental, medical, psychosocial, and school history. Barkley (1990) provides a helpful structured interview format for collecting this information from parents of disruptive children. The interview is conducted chronologically, beginning with prenatal factors and ending with current presenting problems.

Getting a clear picture of presenting problems is critical for establishing treatment goals and selecting the most appropriate intervention. Unfortunately, in the absence of direction from the therapist, parents of disruptive children often express their frustrations and offer only vague descriptions of the child's problem behaviors. When asked about these behaviors, parents may say, "He's just a brat!," "She's mean," "He has an attitude problem," "He won't settle down," and "She wants to control everybody." Although it may be cathartic for parents to vent their frustration, vague descriptions of presenting problems do not easily lend themselves to the formulation of treatment goals. Thus, the therapist must be directive in teaching parents how to use operational definitions of observable behaviors. This can be accomplished by having parents describe presenting complaints as if they were viewing them on a videotape. Parents can be coached to use their "videotalk" to assist the therapist in defining treatment goals (Levy, 1995). Table 5-1 presents examples of vague presenting complaints translated into operational definitions using this technique.

Child Interview. Conducting effective interviews with young children is challenging and requires special skills. There are a number of books and chapters available to assist clinicians with child interviewing. We particularly recommend Hughes and Baker (1990) and Kanfer, Eyberg, and Krahn (1992). The interviewing process can be facilitated by the inclusion of projective techniques such as kinetic family drawings, sentence completion tasks, and thematic storytelling (e.g., Hughes & Baker, 1990; Knell, 1993).

Rating Scales. Although interviewing procedures offer a wealth of important clinical information, the intake evaluation must include quantifiable data as well. Without quantifiable data collected both before and after therapy, it is difficult to provide objective documentation of treatment effectiveness. Quantifiable data may be generated through psychological testing (e.g., intelligence and achievement testing), behavioral observations (e.g., percent of time on-

Table 5-1. Operationalizing Presenting Complaints

Vague	Observable ("Videotalk")
He's so unhappy.	He begins crying over minor disappointments such as someone eating the last popsicle. He never wants to do anything but sit in front of the television.
She's driving me crazy. I can't stand to be around her anymore.	She follows me everywhere and won't even let me go to the bathroom by myself. She whines constantly.
She's not handling our divorce very well.	Last week, she kicked me and said it was my fault that her father left us. She says she doesn't have homework when she really does, and her grades at school are dropping.
He's having trouble accepting the new baby.	He wants to crawl up in my lap and asks for a bottle. When he kisses the baby, it starts out gentle but then he opens his mouth and leaves bite marks.
She's got an attitude!	When I tell her to do something, she tells me to shut up. She says she hates me. She always bosses the other children around, telling them how to play. They get mad and go home.

task in a classroom), and rating scales.

Rating scales are the most commonly used measures of treatment outcome. The most valuable rating scales are those that are standardized with norms that are applicable for the child's age and gender. Normative information offers several advantages to clinicians. First, they may be used to determine whether the severity of presenting problems is outside normal limits. If so, a strong case for the need for treatment may be made to third-party reimbursors. Second, pre- and post-treatment scores can be compared, to document that the child's presenting problems improved. In many cases, the clinician may be able to document changes from outside normal limits before treatment to within normal limits after therapy. This provides compelling evidence of treatment effectiveness which can be communicated to parents, managed care and other funding agencies, and referral sources. If pre- to post-treatment comparisons indicate smaller magnitude improvements, the data may be used to support the clinician's appeal to receive reimbursement for additional sessions.

Perhaps the most widely used parent-report rating scale for children is the Child Behavior Checklist (CBCL; Achenbach, 1991; 1992). Versions are available for two to three-year-old children and for children between the ages of 4 and 18. Parents are asked to rate the frequency of occurrence of approximately 125 common childhood problems. Summary scores are obtained for scales reflecting internalizing problems (e.g., withdrawn, anxious/depressed, somatic complaints) and externalizing problems (e.g., aggressive behavior, delinquent behavior, attention problems). We find this rating scale particularly useful for disruptive children referred for play therapy because treatment goals often address a combination of internalizing and externalizing complaints. A parallel version of the CBCL also is available which may be completed by teachers. The CBCL may be ordered from University Associates in Psychiatry, 1 South Prospect Street, Burlington, VT 05401-3456 (802-656-8313).

A second parent-report rating scale that we typically include in our pretreatment evaluation is the Eyberg Child Behavior Inventory (ECBI; Eyberg, 1992). The ECBI is an empirically-validated, brief measure of disruptive child behavior that is appropriate for use with children ages two and older. The Intensity Score provides an estimate of how frequently the child displays each of 36 problem behaviors, and the Problem Score allows the parent to rate whether or not he or she perceives the behavior to be difficult to manage. To obtain the Intensity Score, the clinician adds up all of the circled frequency scores (i.e., 1 to 7) for the 36 items. To obtain the Problem Score, the clinician simply totals the number of items circled "yes." Children are considered to be rated within the "conduct problem range" when they receive Intensity Scores greater than 127 and/or Problem Scores greater than 11.

The ECBI is particularly useful for identifying parents who may have inappropriately high or inappropriately low expectations for their children's behavior. For example, one mother we worked with reported that she considered 20 of 36 behaviors to be problems for her to handle. However, the frequency with which the child displayed these behaviors was well within normal limits, suggesting that this mother may have had little tolerance for the normal but sometimes irritating behaviors displayed by young children. In contrast, we worked with an overly tolerant father who reported that his son frequently engaged in a large number of disruptive behaviors, but he indicated that he considered none of them to be problems. He expressed the attitude that "boys will be boys," and he felt that his wife and his son's preschool teacher were overreacting to his son's disruptive behavior. The ECBI is reprinted in the Appendix and may be photocopied for clinical and research use.

The Sutter-Eyberg Student Behavior Inventory (SESBI; Eyberg, 1992) is similar in format to the ECBI but is completed by teachers. Intensity Scores greater than 147 and Problem Scores greater than 14 are suggestive of significant conduct problems in the classroom setting. The teachers that we work with especially appreciate the brevity of the SESBI, as it can be completed in approximately five minutes. The SESBI is reprinted in the Appendix and may be photocopied for clinical and research use.

In addition to parent- and teacher-report scales, we find it helpful to include one or more child-report measures. These generally are most appropriate for school-age children who have the requisite cognitive development to provide meaningful responses. Although parent-report information about depression is available on the CBCL, children can be better informants concerning their own affective states. The Children's Depression Inventory (Kovacs, 1985; 1992) is a standardized measure appropriate for children between the ages of 7 and 17 years (it may be ordered by calling 1-800-456-3003). Children are presented with groups of three sentences and are asked to indicate which of the three describes them best over the previous two weeks (e.g., "I am sad once in a while. I am sad many times. I am sad all the time.") Another standardized, child-report measure of emotional functioning is the State-Trait Anxiety Inventory for Children (Spielberger, 1973). Children respond to two inventories with 20 items each. One inventory addresses current feelings of anxiety or state anxiety, and the other addresses general (cross-situational) anxiety or trait anxiety.

A third child-report measure commonly included in our intake assessment battery is the Harter Pictorial Scale of Perceived Competence and Social Acceptance for Young Children (Harter & Pike, 1984). The Harter measures self-esteem in each of the following areas: (a) cognitive competence, (b) physical competence, (c) peer acceptance, and (d) maternal acceptance. Children are presented with a picture of two children and are read a brief statement about them. For example, a child is told that the girl on the left is good at puzzles but the girl on the right is not very good at puzzles. The child is asked to pick which of the two girls she is most like. She is then asked to indicate whether she is a lot like that girl (by pointing to a large circle) or just a little bit like that girl (by pointing to a small circle). The Harter is normed for boys and girls from preschool through second grade. Another version is available for older children as well. The Harter is available from the University of Denver and may be obtained by telephoning 1-303-871-2478.

Translating Intake Information into Play Therapy Goals. Based on the results of the intake evaluation, the evaluator makes a determination regarding the most appropriate treatment. When short-term play therapy has been identified as the treatment of choice, we recommend that the therapist devise a tentative list of treatment goals before the first play therapy session. This list is developed by translating the "videotalk" description of presenting complaints into obtainable and measurable treatment goals. Because this is a short-term intervention, only realistic and circumscribed goals are selected. The list of goals is intended to be a working document, subject to revision and input from the family. Table 5-2 presents sample short-term play therapy goals and corresponding methods of measuring progress.

Table 5-2. Sample Short-Term Play Therapy Goals

Goal	Measurement Method
Displays higher self-esteem	Observations (by parents and therapist) of child's use of positive self-statements Harter Pictorial Scale of Perceived Competence and Social Acceptance in Young Children
Increases use of affective labels	Observations (by parents and therapist) of child's use of "I feel. . ." statements
Demonstrates improved ability to enter a group	CBCL Social Problems Scale Observations (by therapist and teacher) of skill usage
Demonstrates decreased sexualized behavior	CBCL Sex Problems Scale
Demonstrates improved mood	Children's Depression Inventory CBCL Anxious/Depressed Scale
Demonstrates decreased anxiety	State-Trait Anxiety Inventory for Children CBCL Anxious/Depressed Scale
Demonstrates increased compliance with instructions	ECBI SESBI CBCL Aggressive Behavior Scale Observation (parent & therapist) of compliance with instructions
Displays less aggression during dental visits	Observation (therapist & dentist) during dental visit

The First Play Therapy Session

Session One lasts approximately 90 minutes. This extended time period is needed to address several procedural issues specific to the initiation of therapy such as the limits of confidentiality and informed consent/assent. As discussed in Chapter Two, we are careful to set only those precedents which we are able to adhere to throughout the course of treatment. Thus, both parents and children are introduced to the structure of short-term play therapy in the first session. The first play therapy session is divided as follows: (a) Check-in (30 minutes), (b) Child's Work (30 minutes), (c) Child's Play (20 minutes), and (d) Check-out (10 minutes).

Check-In

The therapy appointment begins with a review of our "client awareness form," which provides detailed information concerning the limits of confidentiality, financial arrangements, cancellation policy, emergency procedures, and consent for treatment. Although a sample form is provided in the Appendix, we recommend that every practitioner/agency seek legal advice prior to adopting a client awareness form. Release of information forms also are obtained at the beginning of the session to allow for communication with allied professionals.

Although children do not have a legal right to confidentiality, progress in play therapy is greatly hindered if the child does not feel safe to disclose sensitive information. During the Check-In period, we discuss with the parents and child the need for confidentiality in the child's individual therapy time. We tell parents that we would like to informally agree that specific information shared by the child during play therapy will not be disclosed to parents without the child's permission. Of course, exceptions to this rule are made when children disclose information that causes the therapist to believe that the child or others are in danger. Although we ask parents to agree to confidentiality regarding specific information, we tell the parents and child that therapy progress is enhanced when parents are given enough general information about therapy to serve as allies in treatment. Thus, parents will receive general feedback each session regarding the work that was accomplished and methods that the parent can use to support the Child's Work at home throughout the week.

To help parents understand how short-term play therapy works, they are educated about the therapeutic value of each of the four components. We tell parents:

> Every one of our play therapy sessions will be divided into four parts. First, we will have a Check-In time with you and your child at the beginning of the session. This is a time for you to share important information that can assist in treatment. For example, you might want to tell me about an award that your child received, or a problem at school, or how your child did on play therapy homework. We will restrict our Check-In time to 10 minutes or less so that we have plenty of time left for your child's play therapy. The second part of the session will be Child's Work. During this time, your child will come with me to the playroom and we will do a variety of therapeutic exercises that will help us meet our goals. We might do things like play special therapeutic games, practice talking about feelings, rehearse skills, and read books about children who have had similar experiences. After we finish Child's Work, we will spend a few minutes in Child's Play. This is a time for your child to use toys and art materials to work through conflicts and experiment with the skills we rehearsed in Child's Work. Therapy will usually be fun for your child; it will seem a lot like play to your child. So that you are aware of the work that is being done and can help with the therapy, we will have a Check-Out time at the end of each session. During Check-Out, we will talk about the work that was accomplished during the session and I may ask you to help your child do some play therapy homework during the week.

Parents should be informed about the course of therapy. The beginning sessions focus on establishing rapport, teaching basic concepts about play therapy, and developing a vocabulary for discussing feelings. The next several sessions are spent on activities directly addressing circumscribed play therapy goals. Toward the end of therapy, the parents will become much more actively involved in the therapy hour. They will receive coaching in play therapy skills, and in preparation for termination, the child's dependence will be transferred from the therapist to the parents. A final termination session will be held in which the therapist and child will review and celebrate play therapy accomplishments.

With only 12 sessions to accomplish our goals, it is critical for the child to attend regularly. If there are long gaps between sessions, valuable session time will be lost in re-teaching previously learned skills and rebuilding rapport. To impress upon parents the importance of continuity, we devote some of the first session's Check-In time to forming an attendance contract. This can be done in either verbal or written form. The following is a sample contract:

> I agree to bring my child to play therapy sessions for the next 11 weeks. If I cannot attend because of illness or a scheduling conflict, I agree to call and reschedule the session as soon as possible, preferably within the same week. I understand that the success of this therapy is dependent upon my child's regular attendance. (See Appendix.)

After the business of the first Check-In is completed, the child is escorted by the therapist to the playroom. To set a positive precedent for transitions, the child is encouraged to walk with the therapist, rather than run ahead (see Chapter Four for strategies to handle uncooperative behavior). Most disruptive children comply readily with therapist directions in this first session. They are not yet familiar with the setting or the therapist and are hesitant to test limits. For this reason, the first session provides an excellent opportunity for establishing routines that promote positive behavior.

Child's Work

We have two primary objectives for our first Child's Work session. Our first objective is to introduce the child to basic concepts about play therapy. We want the child to understand what a play therapist is, how play therapy can help children, what kinds of things we do in play therapy, and how confidentiality works. We recommend communicating these concepts through the use of a book entitled *A Child's First Book About Play Therapy* (Nemiroff & Annunziata, 1990). During the first play therapy session, we spend approximately 15 minutes reading this book along with the child. It typically requires two Child's Work sessions to cover all of the material in the book which is relevant to introducing play therapy concepts (excluding termination issues). We choose not to read the section on termination of play therapy until later in treatment.

After reading the book together, we spend the balance of Child's Work addressing our second objective for this session: establishing playroom rules and behavioral expectations. We begin this process by teaching children how to be good listeners. (For a description of how to teach listening skills, please see Chapter Four). Once this skill has been taught, the child can be prompted to use good listening while playroom rules are introduced. Children are told the following rules: (a) Play gently with the toys, (b) No hurting, (c) No leaving the room without permission, and (d) We always work before we play. Children are taught that once the play therapy session begins, they will have an opportunity to get a drink and go to the bathroom only between Child's Work and Child's Play. In addition, we explain and model for the child the ignoring consequence for disruptive behavior (see Chapter Four).

As stated above, we prefer to begin our Child's Work by introducing play therapy concepts before addressing playroom rules. This is ideal because it allows for some rapport building prior to limit-setting. Some children with short attention spans and highly disruptive behavior, however, are unable to participate appropriately in the reading of the book without clear limits.

For these children, we suspend reading the book until they have been taught the listening skills and playroom rules.

Child's Play

After completing the Child's Work portion of the session, children are told that it is time to take their bathroom and drink break. During the break, materials appropriate for use during Child's Play are brought into the playroom. We typically leave the Child's Work materials out during the Child's Play portion should the child choose to continue this activity during Child's Play. In this first session, the therapist spends approximately 20 minutes in child-directed play. (For a description of child-directed play, please see Chapter Two.) Because precedents are set in the first session, it is important that the therapist establish the routine for ending Child's Play that will be used in all subsequent sessions. (For a complete description of rituals for ending Child's Play, including transition statements and clean up, please see Chapter Two). Prior to Check-Out, the therapist also discusses with the child whether or not specific child-initiated content will be shared with the parent during Check-Out.

Check-Out

The last 10 minutes of the first play therapy session is spent in Check-Out with the parents and the child. The therapist takes this opportunity to provide specific praise about how hard the child worked. This strategy helps to build rapport with the family, motivating both the child and the parent to work hard in therapy. Parents are informed in a general way about what material was covered in the session and the therapist repeats to the parent the playroom rules. Parents can then support the behavioral expectations outlined by the therapist and the child is given another opportunity to learn the rules. Because a primary objective of the session involves teaching play therapy concepts to both the parents and the child, the family is given a homework assignment to read the play therapy book together several times during the week. They are asked to read only the section of the book that was read with the therapist during Child's Work. We simply mark the page with a paper clip. For homework assignments, we send home an inexpensive black and white booklet version of *A Child's First Book About Play Therapy* (available from the American Psychological Association, 1-800-374-2721).

The Second Play Therapy Session

Session Two is conducted in a typical 60-minute session format. Similar to the first play therapy appointment, a primary objective of Session Two is to teach both the parent and child about the structure and process of play therapy. First, play therapy concepts are reviewed, and those not covered in session one are introduced. Second, playroom rules and behavioral expectations are reviewed and reinforced. The therapist remains vigilant for instances in which the child follows the new rules and promptly responds with labeled praises and/or stickers.

During a 10-minute Check-In, the therapist inquires about completion of the homework assignment (i.e., reading the play therapy book). It is important to set the precedent in this session that parents always will be held accountable for doing their homework. During the 20-minute Child's Work session, listening skills and playroom rules will be reviewed. Then, the therapist will continue to read the play therapy book with the child (except for the termination section), and an exercise will be conducted on age-appropriate labels for feelings (e.g., "Ups and Downs with Feelings" cards). Approximately 20 minutes of the session is spent in Child's Play. The therapist allows the child to lead the play and uses play therapy process skills to enhance rapport and strengthen child self-esteem. To end the session, a 10-minute Check-Out is conducted with the parents and the child. The child is encouraged to demonstrate identification of feeling labels for the parent. A homework assignment is given for the parent to assist the child in labeling age-appropriate feelings (e.g., "happy," "sad," "angry," and "scared" for three-to six-year-old children). To encourage compliance with the homework assignment, parents are given a recording sheet to keep track of homework completion.

6

THE MIDDLE STAGE OF THERAPY: SESSIONS THREE THROUGH SEVEN

Children referred for short-term play therapy have diverse presenting problems. For example, they may enter therapy because they have experienced a traumatic stressor, have difficulties with chronic anxiety or depression, or have skill deficiencies. Play therapists also are diverse with respect to the types of populations they work with and the types of interventions they are comfortable employing. For these reasons, it is not possible nor desirable for this chapter to provide a cookbook approach to the middle stages of treatment. Instead, we encourage therapists to use the short-term play therapy framework flexibly, drawing upon their own creativity and experiences in tailoring the techniques to address individualized treatment goals.

In the third through seventh sessions, we strongly recommend that therapists adhere to the established play therapy sequence: Check-In, Child's Work, Child's Play, and Check-Out. Additionally, it is important that therapists consistently use the play therapy process skills and behavior management strategies described in Chapters Three and Four (e.g., description, imitation, praise, strategic ignoring, giving good directions, contingent attention). Precedents and routines established in the first two play therapy sessions must be maintained throughout this stage of treatment. By preserving the structure, process skills, and precedents, valuable therapy time is not lost in unsuccessful attempts to manage increasingly disruptive behavior. Thus, more therapy time and therapist energy is available for the goal-directed work of Sessions Three through Seven.

Forming a Treatment Plan

When we first began doing play therapy, it was widely understood that nondirective play therapy was a slow and gradual process and that the child guided the content and pace of each session. The therapist's role was to facilitate this process by providing a safe, nurturing environment full of toys and materials. We often did little planning before sessions because it was the child's job to select activities and lead the play. In longer-term play therapy, efficiency was not a priority and there could be many sessions in which goal-directed themes were not evident.

In short-term play therapy, efficiency is critical because the therapist has a limited number of sessions to effect change. Each session must produce progress toward identified treatment goals, with the content of each session building upon the previous one. We can no longer enter sessions without a clear and integrated plan for how the time can be used most efficiently to meet treatment goals. The therapist must pre-plan the content and activities to ensure that all treatment goals are adequately addressed. In our short-term play therapy approach, a flexible but detailed treatment plan is generated prior to the beginning of session three.

Developing a treatment plan involves three steps. First, the tentative list of treatment goals devised with parental input in the first treatment session is reviewed and prioritized. In a short-term play therapy approach, it is generally feasible to address no more than three specific goals. Once these goals have been determined, the second step is to generate a list of goal-directed Child's Work activities. These activities may be designed by the therapist (see Chapter Two) or based upon commercially-available products. Listings of popular play therapy tools are provided in Table 6-1. The Child's Work activities should be ordered in such a way that skills and content learned in early sessions form a foundation for more advanced work in later sessions. The third step in forming the treatment plan is to develop homework assignments that support the work conducted in play therapy. A sample worksheet is provided in the Appendix that will assist in the formulation of a session-by-session treatment plan.

Tables 6-2 and 6-3 show sample treatment plans for the middle stage of therapy that were devised prior to the third play therapy session. Pre-established plans such as these must be used flexibly. Children may accomplish goals more or less quickly than therapists anticipate, and adjustments should be made accordingly. As treatment progresses, the need for new goals can become apparent as children feel safe in disclosing sensitive information. Even during the course of a short-term treatment, new problems and issues can arise (e.g., death of a family member, expulsion from school, placement in a foster home) requiring an adjustment in the treatment plan. We recommend that progress toward treatment goals be monitored on a session-by-session basis.

Table 6-1. Commercially-Available Play Therapy Products

TITLE	FORMAT
DIVORCE	
All About Divorce	Book
My Life Turned Upside Down, But I Turned it Rightside Up	Book
My Two Homes	Game
The Changing Family Game	Game
Let's Talk: Early Separation and Divorce Activity Book	Book
My Story: Divorce and Remarriage Activity Book	Book
FEELING IDENTIFICATION	
Talking, Feeling, and Doing Game	Game
All Feelings Are OK	Workbook
Face-It Card Deck	Game
Face Your Feelings!	Workbook
The Great Feelings Chase	Game
Feeling Dolls	Dolls
Dealing with Feelings Card Game	Game
Feelings Hand Puppets	Puppets
The Feelings Game	Game
My Ups and Downs	Cards
Blast-Off! The Kids' Game About Feelings	Game
Ups and Downs with Feelings	Game
The Magic Map of Feelings	Game
PREPARATION FOR COURT	
Kids' Day in Court	Game
Chris Tells the Truth	Book
ADOPTION	
The Adoption Story Cards	Cards
SELF-ESTEEM	
The Building Blocks of Self-Esteem	Workbook
The Dinosaur's Journey to High Self-Esteem	Game
Don't Feed the Monster on Tuesdays!	Book
How to Be a Super-Hero	Workbook
Let's See. . . About Me	Game
Let's See. . . About Me	Workbook
My Best Friend is Me!	Book
The Self-Concept Game	Game
10 Steps to Feeling Good About Yourself	Poster
The Self-Esteem Game	Game
Feeling Good About Yourself	Workbook
SEXUAL AND PHYSICAL ABUSE	
My Body is Mine, My Feelings Are Mine	Book
No More Hurt	Workbook
My Own Thoughts on Stopping the Hurt	Workbook
Play it Safe. . . With SASA	Game
Be Safe. . . Be Aware!	Game
It's MY Body	Book
The Trouble with Secrets	Book

Table 6-1. (continued)

Kelly Bear Feelings	Book
Something is Wrong at My House	Book
Something Happened and I'm Scared to Tell	Book

STRESS

Take a Deep Breath	Workbook
Don't Pop Your Cork on Mondays!	Book
Stress Strategies	Game
Dinosaurs Get Stress, Too!	Game
Stress Attack	Game

SOCIAL AND COMMUNICATION SKILLS

Communicate Junior	Game
Getting Along	Book/Audiotape
Let's See. . . About Me and My Friends	Game
Let's See. . . About Me and My Friends	Workbook
The Social Skills Game	Game
The Anger Control Game	Game

SIBLING ISSUES

Baby and I Can Play	Book
Fun with Toddlers	Book
Let's See. . . About Me and My Family	Game
Let's See. . . About Me and My Family	Workbook

GRIEF

When Someone Very Special Dies	Workbook
The Goodbye Game	Game

For information regarding the publishers, authors, and/or purchase of these materials, please contact Childswork/Childsplay (1-800-962-1141) or the Creative Therapy Store (1-800-648-8857).

Table 6-2. Treatment Plan for Decreasing Fear Behaviors in a Dog Phobic: The Middle Stage of Therapy

Session #	Child's Work Activity	Homework Assignment
3	Tape-record relaxation training session	Listen to relaxation tape each day
4	Construct a fear hierarchy Have child relax while therapist reads a book about a dog	Listen to relaxation tape while looking at a book about dogs
5	Expose child to early steps on hierarchy while practicing relaxation (e.g., stuffed animal, puppy in a cage)	Invite child to watch while family members play with a friendly puppy
6	Continue to expose child to steps on hierarchy while relaxing (touching puppy, listening to barking sound on tape recorder)	Invite child to join in while family members play with a friendly puppy
7	Expose child to last step on hierarchy while relaxing (big, safe dog) Read termination section of *A Child's First Book About Play Therapy*	Continue offering opportunities for exposure to dogs Read termination section of play therapy book

Table 6-3. Treatment Plan for Reducing Anger Associated with Visits to Non-Custodial Parent: The Middle Stage of Therapy

Session	Child's Work Activity	Homework Assignment
3	"Talking, Feeling, and Doing Game" (using cards with family themes)	Practice "I feel. . ." statements before bedtime
4	Use chalkboard to present basic divorce concepts (dividing household into two) Make Kinetic Family Drawings of Two Families Review therapeutic book about divorce (e.g., *All About Divorce* or *My Life Turned Upside Down, But I Turned It Rightside Up*)	Read divorce book twice
5	Play therapeutic game about divorce (e.g., "My Two Homes")	Read divorce book twice
6	Play therapeutic game about divorce (e.g., "My Two Homes") Discuss ways that child can better cope with transition from father's to mother's home	Convene family meeting to discuss ways to help child cope better with transitions
7	Role-play ways to communicate with parents about feelings related to divorce Read termination section of *A Child's First Book About Play Therapy*	Implement transition ideas prior to next visit Read termination section of play therapy book

Case Example

To illustrate the selection of goal-directed activities in Sessions Three through Seven, we will present the case of "Brian." Brian is an eight-year-old-boy who was referred for treatment of sexualized behavior subsequent to chronic sexual abuse. Specific behavioral concerns included touching other children's private parts, masturbating in the presence of others, and being indiscriminately affectionate. Brian's foster mother completed the Child Behavior Checklist and Brian received clinically elevated ratings on the Sex Problems, Aggressive Behavior, and Anxious/Depressed Scales.

Sessions One and Two. In the first two sessions, Brian was introduced to basic concepts of play therapy and the use of affective labels. When reading *A Child's First Book About Play Therapy,* Brian was asked what problems he had that could be worked on in play therapy. Not surprisingly, he did not volunteer his sexualized behavior as a problem. The therapist commented that Brian's mother had already talked about how Brian sometimes had a problem knowing when it is okay to touch his own private parts and other children's private parts. The therapist went on to say that although Brian did not have to talk about that in his first session, it would be discussed later in play therapy.

Session Three. Child's Work began with the following statement from the therapist: "Brian, do you remember a couple of weeks ago when we looked at the play therapy book? I told you then that sometime we would talk about touching private parts. Today we are going to begin talking a little bit about that. But first, let's draw some pictures together." Brian was asked to draw one picture of a boy and one picture of a girl. These pictures were used to illustrate the concept of private parts. The therapist explained that private parts are all of the parts of the body that are covered by a boy's swimming trunks and a girl's bikini. These concepts were further reinforced by having Brian use a different crayon to draw a bathing suit on each of the figures. During Child's Play, Brian spontaneously picked up a Barbie doll and showed the therapist the location of the doll's private parts. The therapist responded by praising Brian for having been a good listener and remembering what he had learned. During Check-out, the foster mother was encouraged to increase her supervision of Brian to prevent opportunities for sexual acting out with other children.

Session Four. During the Check-In, the foster mother was shown a book about appropriate sexual behavior and was asked how she felt about Brian seeing this book. With her consent, the book *It's My Body* (Freeman, 1982) was read with Brian during Child's Work. The therapist also used the pictures that Brian made in Session Three to review the concept of private parts. Brian chose to play with Legos during Child's Play, and the therapist followed his lead. He appeared to enjoy playing with the therapist and asked, "When do I get to come back again?" At Check-Out time, the therapist and Brian explained the concepts of good and bad touch to Brian's foster mother. Brian was praised for demonstrating what he had learned, and his foster mother was pleased that the sexualized behavior was being targeted directly in therapy. The foster mother was given a homework assignment to further reinforce these concepts by reviewing them with Brian and praising him for touching family members and peers appropriately.

Session Five. After reviewing the homework assignment with Brian and his foster mother during Check-In, the Child's Work portion of the session again focused on good and bad touches. The book *It's My Body* was completed, and an exercise was conducted at the chalkboard. The chalkboard was divided into three segments: one for good touches (e.g., gentle hand holding) and one for each of the two types of bad touches (i.e., aggression and touching private parts). Brian was asked to generate examples of each type of touching. Once the board was full, the therapist asked Brian to erase the bad touch segments. Family puppets were used to role-play the different types of touches and appropriate responses when someone wants to touch a child's private parts. Brian was encouraged to practice with the puppets assuming both the roles of the victim and perpetrator. As a metaphor, Brian was taught that interpersonal space is like "a bubble." He was told:

> When you get too close to someone you can pop the bubble, and people feel yucky when their bubbles get popped. So that people won't feel yucky, it is important to ask permission before you give hugs or kisses. If they give you permission, they can make their bubbles smaller so they won't pop when you hug each other.

During Child's Play, Brian was praised for respecting the therapist's bubble, and the therapist used puppets to model how to ask before invading Brian's bubble (e.g., "Could I have a hug?") Puppets were used for modeling the hug as we feel that therapists should avoid hugging children in individual therapy. During Check-Out, Brian's foster mother was introduced to the bubble metaphor. Her homework assignment was to prompt and reinforce Brian for respecting the bubbles of others.

Session Six. Prior to Session Six, the therapist telephoned the foster mother to discuss some sensitive information about dealing with masturbation. The therapist explained that an effective treatment strategy would be to begin restricting masturbation to private settings. The foster mother was given an opportunity to share her thoughts and feelings about this approach. When the foster mother agreed with this strategy, the therapist obtained specific information about the settings in which self-stimulation would and would not be allowed. During the Child's Work portion of Session Six, the puppet role-plays were continued. The therapist talked with Brian about the times and settings in which it is acceptable to touch one's own private parts. Brian was told that masturbation is a private activity in the same way that using the restroom is done privately. He was also told that people feel uncomfortable watching someone do a private activity. A doll house was used to demonstrate the areas of the house in which masturbation is acceptable. Role-plays with doll house figures were used to help Brian understand the rules for touching one's private parts. During Child's Play, Brian chose to continue doll house play, but no sexual themes were evident. Brian was asked whether it would be alright with him if the therapist discussed today's work with the foster mother (specifically, issues regarding appropriate places to engage in private activities). He provided his consent. During Check-Out, the therapist and foster mother outlined a plan for prompting and redirecting Brian when he engaged in self-stimulation in inappropriate settings. The foster mother was encouraged to continue prompting and praising Brian for respecting other's interpersonal space.

Session Seven. After homework was reviewed with the family, a therapeutic game called "Be Safe. . . Be Aware!" was played with Brian during the Child's Work portion of Session Seven. To prepare Brian for upcoming termination, the remainder of *A Child's First Book About Play Therapy* was read. Feelings about loss and saying "goodbye" were discussed. In Child's Play, Brian chose to continue playing the "Be Safe. . . Be Aware!" game. While walking to the Check-Out room, Brian asked the therapist for a hug. The therapist responded, "I'm very proud of you for not breaking my bubble! You remembered to ask before touching me. Here (holds hand out), I would prefer to shake your hand. I like shaking hands with you." During Check-Out, the foster mother was encouraged to continue redirecting inappropriate self-stimulation, to praise Brian for respecting interpersonal space, and to read the termination section of Brian's copy of *A Child's First Book About Play Therapy.*

Preparing for Termination

In short-term treatment approaches, families must begin preparation for termination after relatively few treatment sessions. In our play therapy, Session Seven is the ideal time to introduce termination themes because it immediately precedes a major shift in treatment. In Session Eight, we begin transferring the child's dependence from the therapist to the parents. Decreasing amounts of time are spent individually with the child, as the parents are coached in play therapy skills. Children must be prepared for the upcoming changes in therapy. Otherwise, they are likely to feel cheated by the parents' intrusion in their individual time with the therapist, and disruptive behavior may increase.

As illustrated in the case of Brian, termination themes are introduced to the child during the Child's Work portion of the seventh session. Once again, we return to *A Child's First Book About Play Therapy*. The termination pages omitted early in treatment are read with the child during the session, and parents are asked to read this section of the book to the child at home. In addition, the therapist explains to the child that something very different will start happening in therapy. Including the parents in Child's Work is presented as a helpful way for the child and therapist to say their "long goodbye" (Nemiroff & Annunziata, 1990). To decrease resistance, it is important to emphasize the fun nature of the "special playtime" that the child will begin sharing with the parent.

7

TEACHING PLAY THERAPY SKILLS TO PARENTS: SESSION EIGHT

A major shift occurs in the eighth play therapy session. Whereas the focus in earlier sessions was on addressing goals through individual work with the child, the later sessions emphasize joint therapy with the child and parent (or other primary caregiver). There are several important reasons for making this shift. First, it facilitates the transfer of dependence from the therapist-child relationship to the longer-term and more primary parent-child relationship. Children are helped to accept termination of treatment when their attachment to the therapist is gradually reduced and replaced with a strengthened parent-child bond. Second, problems associated with the parent-child relationship are central to many presenting complaints. This is highlighted when working with children with disruptive behavior problems who typically engage in coercive interactional patterns with their parents. Yet, it can be seen with other presenting problems as well. In her work with sexually abused girls, Long (1986) recognizes the need to strengthen mother-child relationships to prevent future molestation and other problems. Similar to our approach, Long (1986) recommends a gradual shift from individual child work to parent-child bonding exercises. A third reason to move toward parent-child work in later sessions is to enhance generalization of treatment effects across settings and over time. Parents can serve as "co-therapists" to promote progress outside the therapy hour.

Beginning in Session Eight of our short-term play therapy approach, parents are taught play therapy skills as a means of improving the parent-child relationship (Eyberg & Boggs, 1989). There are several similarities between the play therapy taught to parents and the process skills used by therapists during Child's Play. Parents are taught to describe the play activity, reflect child verbalizations, imitate, and praise. As is the case in Child's Play, primary goals of the parent's play therapy include improving child self-esteem, enhancing the relationship, and managing minor disruptive behavior through the use of contingent attention. Yet, there are key differences between the form of play therapy taught to parents and the form used by therapists. Because they are not mental health professionals, parents do not have either the training or the objectivity to employ interpretative skills. Parents are also not prepared to formulate treatment plans and utilize specialized therapeutic techniques, like those used in Child's Work. Thus, processing affectively-laden material and helping children to gain insight are not goals of the play therapy employed by parents.

When No Caregiver is Available

Often it is difficult to enlist the assistance of caregivers in child therapy. In some settings, it is common for parents or foster parents to drop their child off for treatment expecting that it is the job of the therapist to "fix" the child's problems. We recognize that it can be difficult to change parental attitudes concerning their role in the therapeutic process. However, even poorly motivated parents can sometimes be engaged in therapy when, from the initial contact, the therapist communicates that parental involvement is essential.

Sometimes, a parent or other primary caregiver is simply not available to participate in the child's treatment. This can occur when children are placed in residential care settings without their primary caregivers. It can also occur when a child is in foster care and the foster parent does not view therapy participation as part of his or her job responsibilities. Some children reside with natural parents who do not have the emotional, intellectual, or environmental resources needed to be effective participants in therapy. These may be parents who are actively abusing substances, not taking their medication for schizophrenia or bipolar disorder, or experiencing catastrophic life events. When a caregiver is unavailable, we recommend that therapists maintain the individual play therapy structure (i.e., Child's Work followed by Child's Play) for the entire course of treatment.

Structuring the Therapy Hour

So that parents can devote their undivided attention to learning play therapy skills, they attend Session Eight without the child. The first ten minutes are spent in Check-In, reviewing the previous week's homework and life events. The next 40 minutes are used to describe, model, and role-play the play therapy skills with the parents. Parents are not passive learners in this process but are encouraged to ask questions, offer examples, and practice skills. We incorporate a repetitive teaching style in which we frequently review previously-taught skills. To help diffuse any performance anxiety that parents may experience, we teach in a casual fashion, making frequent use of humor. The last 10 minutes are spent in Check-Out. The parents are given a homework assignment to complete before the next session.

Overview and Rationale

Parents are told that they will be taught a set of play therapy skills to use with their child in a daily 5- to 10-minute play session. To help them understand the purpose of this "special playtime," they are told that they can assist treatment progress by serving as co-therapists. Parents are encouraged to value the therapeutic nature of the special playtime and to view it as something qualitatively different from ordinary play. They are told that the child will be in the lead and they will follow along at their child's level of development. By making play child-directed and providing undivided attention, the parent sets the child up for good behavior. This, in turn, makes it easier for the parent to communicate approval and establish a more positive relationship with the child. Special playtime goals that are individualized for the family's presenting problems are discussed. Examples of goals that might be applicable to a particular family include increasing child self-esteem, decreasing anger, improving social skills, developing constructive play skills, strengthening family relationships, and using words to communicate feelings.

Many parents think that if 5 minutes are good, then 30 must be better. The therapist should warn parents that this will be an intensive five minutes requiring good concentration and a high energy level. Goals can be accomplished adequately in five to ten minutes, and longer play sessions tend to burn parents out. It is more therapeutic to provide shorter play sessions that children can count on daily than to provide sporadic but longer play sessions.

Parents also are reminded that because one of the goals of special playtime is to strengthen the parent-child relationship, it is important that each parent do special playtime individually with their child each day.

Parents are warned that a great deal of information will be presented in the session and that they are not expected to become good "play therapists" overnight. Instead, significant portions of the next three sessions will be devoted to direct coaching of special playtime skills. Parents are told that a handout with definitions and examples of the skills will be given to them at the end of the session and that they need not worry about taking notes (please see Appendix for "Do" and "Don't" Skills for Special Playtime Parent Handout on play therapy skills).

The "Don't" Skills

When conducting special playtime, we ask parents to refrain from using directions, questions, and criticism (please see Table 7-1 for a summary of the special playtime rules). Because the overriding rule of special playtime is that the child remain in the lead, parents are discouraged from giving directions and suggestions. A direction is a declarative statement telling the child what to do. Examples include, "Hand me the block," "Put a red one on next," "Sit in the chair," and "Pick a toy to play with." A suggestion is a question which more subtly takes the child's lead away. The following are examples of suggestions: "Would you hand me a block, please?" "How about putting the red one on next?" "Why don't you sit down on the chair?" and "Do you want to pick a toy to play with?" With disruptive children, both suggestions and directions set the stage for an unpleasant power struggle should the child choose not to comply.

Table 7-1. The "Don't" and "Do" Skills for Special Playtime

Don't. . .	Do. . .
Give directions	Describe
Ask questions	Reflect
Criticize	Imitate
	Praise
	Ignore disruptive behavior

Parents are also discouraged from asking questions during special playtime. They are told that questions take the lead away in a conversation by influencing what the child is to talk about. Most questions start with an interrogative word such as, "who," "what," "when," "where," "how," "why," or "which." Other questions are communicated via voice inflection (e.g., "That's a doggy?") or by adding a short phrase, or tag, to the end of a statement (e.g, "That's a house, isn't it?") We explain to parents that questions are not a poor communication skill. There are many times throughout the day when it is important for parents to ask children questions. Unfortunately, parents tend to overuse questions with young children, causing children to feel interrogated and overwhelmed. To illustrate how questions can discourage children from talking during playtime, the following common example is provided:

Child: "I'm making a boat."
Parent: "What kind of boat is it? Is it a sailboat or a motorboat? Who is driving the boat? Can I sail with you? Where are we going? Are we going to an island?"
Child: [feels overwhelmed and tunes parent out]

In this example the questions are provided in a rapid-fire fashion, providing the child with no opportunity to either answer or initiate further conversation. For most parents, avoiding questions is the hardest of all of the special playtime skills, as it requires modification of a well-ingrained habit.

The third type of verbalization that parents are taught to avoid is criticism. Criticism is defined as any comment that expresses unfavorable judgement about a quality of the child or a child's play product. Obviously, parents are to avoid using such blatant criticisms as, "That's stupid," "You're not being very nice," and "That will never work." They also are taught to avoid correcting children in a critical way. For example, children may feel criticized when parents say, "No, that's not a square. It's a rectangle." A less critical way to provide corrective feedback is to leave off the negative part and simply say, "It's a rectangle." Finally, parents are asked to avoid criticism intended to prohibit misbehavior, such as directions including the words "no," "don't," "stop," and "quit."

We encourage parents to refrain from criticizing because it detracts from the warmth of the interaction and takes a toll on children's self-esteem. Disruptive and highly active children are criticized more often than peers due to their higher rate of irritating and intrusive behaviors. To help parents understand the detrimental impact of criticism on young children, Hembree-Kigin and McNeil (1995) present the following explanation:

> Young children do not have the cognitive development to be able to think critically and independently. Their attitudes and beliefs are heavily influenced by the things that adults tell them, particularly statements made by trusted adults like parents. If a parent tells a preschool child that "horses fly" then as far as the child is concerned, horses do fly. Most preschoolers do not have the ability to hear this statement, think back on what a horse looks like, realize that wings are needed to fly, recognize that horses have no wings, and come to the conclusion that their trusted parent has made an error. Similarly, if a parent tells a preschool girl she is dumb, then the girl incorporates that information into her self-image without scrutiny. She does not have the cognitive sophistication to think back to earlier in the day when she was successful at putting together a difficult ten piece puzzle and realize that the parent is wrong and she is pretty smart after all. (p. 32)

A second reason to avoid criticism is that it may increase rather than decrease disruptive behavior. Many disruptive behaviors are attempts to obtain stimulating attention. When parents respond by expressing displeasure, they inadvertently reward the child for the misbehavior. Whereas a child with a calm and cooperative temperament is likely to respond to criticism by feeling remorseful and discontinuing the behavior, an oppositional child is likely to enjoy the attention and to escalate the misbehavior. Parents are asked to consider the following example:

> Suppose that your son is sitting on the couch with you and feeling restless and bored. He kicks off his shoes, puts his feet on you and says, "Ooh, my feet stink." To get him to stop, you respond with a criticism such as, "Don't do that. You're being gross." What is your son likely to do next? That's right! He's likely to keep his feet on you and

maybe even move them closer to your face. So, your criticism didn't work. In fact, it made the situation even worse.

The "Do" Skills

After hearing about all of the "don't" skills, parents are left wondering what is left to say or do during the playtime. There are four primary "do" skills: describe, reflect, imitate, and praise (see Table 7-1). A helpful mnemonic for remembering the "do" skills is the acronym "DRIP."

Parents are taught to describe their child's appropriate behavior. Description is a running commentary on the child's play, much like a sportscaster offering a play-by-play account of the child's activities. As the child builds with blocks, the parent might say, "You're putting the red block on top of the blue one. Oh, you made a bridge! Now the cars are driving over the bridge." Descriptions communicate to the child that the parent is interested in the activity and is devoting his or her undivided attention. If the parent is describing the child's activity, he or she cannot be distracted by extraneous thoughts like what will be prepared for dinner. Descriptions make the play more exciting for children and help them to stay with one activity for increasingly longer periods of time. Planning skills are enhanced as children learn to describe their own activities, both aloud and silently in their minds. Parents are taught to be selective in their descriptions, commenting only on positive and neutral behaviors. The rationale for this is that descriptions provide attention and serve to increase the described behavior. Therefore, a parent should not describe her son's action of tossing the giraffe across the room, because to do so would reinforce his disruptive play and would likely result in throwing of other toys.

The second "do" skill is to reflect appropriate speech. A reflection is a repetition of the child's words. The simplest reflection is one in which the parent reflects the child's comment exactly. So, if a child says, "The cat is driving the car," the parent can reflect, "Yes, the cat is driving the car." Alternatively, the parent can provide a reflection that expands upon the child's comments. This type of "elaborative reflection" shows that the parent is listening to the child and adds interest value to the comment. In the above example, an elaborative reflection would be, "The purple cat is driving the car around the house." Developmentally, it is preferable to use elaborative reflections with older children, as direct repetition of their words can seem patronizing. See Table 7-2 for examples of reflective statements.

Reflections are a powerful way to enhance communication between parents and children. They make it clear to children that parents are interested in their thoughts, feelings, and opinions. Parental reflection serves to reward children's speech, resulting in increased verbal expression. Unlike questions, reflections stimulate communication without leading the conversation. It is important for parents to learn to reflect with certainty, eliminating question words and intonation. When a child says something like, "This is a ghost buggy," parents must work hard to avoid the reflexive tendency to respond with a question (e.g., "Is that a ghost buggy?" or "A ghost buggy?") Such a question leads children to think that the parent was not listening carefully or did not agree with the child. In contrast, if the parent reflects the comment with a definitive statement such as, "That is a ghost buggy," the child is likely to feel understood and validated. As is the case with all of the "do" skills, parents should only reflect appropriate verbalizations. A "whiney" statement such as, "These toys are boring," should be ignored rather than reflected because a reflection would reinforce and probably increase the whining.

Table 7-2. Reflecting Children's Speech

Child: *"This girl is going roller skating."*
Parent: *"The little girl is going roller skating."*

Child: *"Look. . . choo-choo."*
Parent: *"You found a choo-choo train."*

Child: *"The sun has a smiley face."*
Parent: *"The sun is feeling happy today."*

Child: *"Pasghetti got ate up."*
Parent: *"Someone was hungry and ate all of the spaghetti."*

Child: *"I'm drawing tears on the pumpkin's face."*
Parent: *"The pumpkin is very sad about something."*

The third "do" skill is to imitate appropriate play. Parents can directly imitate by playing exactly like the child plays. If the child draws a circle, the parent says, "I'm going to draw a circle just like yours." This type of imitation is very appealing to younger children who feel special and appreciated when imitated. With older children, it is better to provide a more subtle version of imitation which involves engaging in a similar activity without copying their exact play. For example, when a ten-year-old builds a car out of blocks, his father can build a road. Imitation is a nonverbal method of providing attention to children that sends a message of approval of the child's choice of activity. With disruptive children, imitation serves the important function of teaching children to share and to take turns. This occurs through a combination of modeling and labeled praise. Consider the following example:

> **Child:** [writes name at top of paper]
> **Parent:** *"I'll grab a sheet of paper also. Thanks for sharing the paper with me. I'm going to write my name at the top of the page like you did."*
> **Child:** *"I'm making a rainbow."*
> **Parent:** *"I'm going to color a rainbow like yours."*
> **Child:** [gathers up the crayons] *"No! I'm playing with the crayons!"*
> **Parent:** [ignores and describes own play] *"I'm drawing some grass."*
> **Child:** *"I made the bumblebee purple."*
> **Parent:** [reflects] *"You did make the bumblebee purple. That's a good idea. I'm going to make a bumblebee also. Thanks for sharing this crayon with me. It's fun to play with you when you share and let me play too."*
> **Child:** *"I need a brown crayon."*
> **Parent:** [models sharing] *"Here. I will share my brown crayon with you."*

An additional benefit of imitating is that it keeps the child in the lead. Rather than making suggestions about how the child could play differently, the parent imitates the child's activities. Imitating is most effective when the parent remains at or below the child's developmental level. Parents should not get carried away and make elaborate log cabin townships while their children are struggling to get one log to fit on top of another.

The fourth, and perhaps most important, of the "do" skills is to praise the child's desirable activities, qualities, and products. Parents are taught about the two types of praise: unlabeled and labeled (please see Chapters Three and Four for more information on praise). Labeled, or specific, praise is considered to be more effective for both self-esteem enhancement and behavior management. It communicates to the child exactly what he or she did to earn parental approval. The following example may be given to help parents understand the differential effectiveness of labeled and unlabeled praise:

> Suppose that your daughter writes the alphabet across a sheet of paper, and you say, "very good." She will enjoy receiving the praise, but she will not know exactly which behavior to continue in order to obtain more praise. Suppose that you choose instead to say, "Very good job of keeping the letters on the line." What is she likely to try to do the next time she writes something? That's right. She will try to keep those letters on the line because she knows that you like that. Consider how her behavior might have changed differently if you had said, "Very good job of holding the pencil with three fingers like the teacher showed you." On the other hand, consider how you would have encouraged an entirely different behavior if you had said, "Very good job of working on your alphabet. I am proud of you when you work hard on school work." You can see how labeled praise can be a very powerful tool for motivating children to behave in certain ways.

Parents are told that praise may be the single best tool for enhancing children's self-esteem. Because children with disruptive behavior problems receive so many criticisms each day, it is a challenge for parents to provide enough praise to counteract the self-esteem damage done by criticism. Special playtime provides an excellent opportunity to praise at a high level. Because the children have their parents' undivided attention and are leading the play, they typically are well-behaved, displaying numerous behaviors worthy of praise. Parents are told that they should strive to praise young children (under the age of seven) approximately 15 times in 5 minutes (i.e., once every 20 seconds). Because of developmental issues which render high rates of praise ineffective with older children (see Chapter Three), parents should emphasize quality rather than quantity when praising a child in the 8- to 12-year-old range. The information in Table 7-3 is reviewed with parents to help them identify and praise their children's positive behavior and attributes.

Managing Disruptive Behavior

Misbehavior during special playtime can be thought of as falling into one of two categories: (1) dangerous/destructive, or (2) annoying/disruptive. Dangerous/destructive behaviors can cause harm to the child or parent or significant damage to property. Examples include kicking, biting, pulling hair, throwing toys, pulling curtains down, writing on walls, and breaking toys. It is uncommon for children to engage in this category of misbehavior during special playtime because no demands are being placed on them and they have their parent's undivided attention. Behaviors falling into the annoying/disruptive category are inappropriate but do not result in harm. Most misbehaviors displayed by children during special playtime fall into this category. Examples include bossiness, whining, using foul language, spitting, teasing, playing roughly with toys, and screaming.

Table 7-3. Mastering Labeled Praise

Sentence Stems for Labeled Praise	Praiseworthy Behaviors/Qualities
I like it when you. . .	try hard
Terrific job. . .	completing that puzzle
I feel proud when you. . .	share toys
Thank you for. . .	using an inside voice
That was nice of you to. . .	play gently with the toys
You are good at. . .	using polite manners
I am glad that you. . .	picked up the toys
It makes me happy when you. . .	sit still in the chair
That was smart to. . .	read the directions
Good idea to. . .	take turns

Parents are taught different strategies for handling the two types of misbehavior. For danger-ous/destructive behavior, parents are told to stop the special playtime. They are encouraged to say something like, "Hurting is not allowed. Special playtime is over for today. We will try again tomorrow." Although parents may choose to provide an additional consequence such as timeout, we find that termination of playtime is often effective for preventing future incidences of dangerous and destructive behavior.

For annoying and/or disruptive behavior, we recommend the use of strategic ignoring. When a child engages in an inappropriate behavior, parents are told to break eye contact with the child immediately and to turn away. It is very important that their facial expression display no reaction to the child's misbehavior. Parents should not show signs of irritation, amuse-ment, or shock. They should continue playing independently with the toys, acting as if they cannot see or hear the child. To distract (or redirect) the child into a more positive behavior, parents should describe their own play in an enthusiastic and creative fashion while ignoring their child. At the first sign that the child is engaging in a neutral or positive behavior, the par-ent should quickly return the attention and provide labeled praise. The following is an exam-ple of the ignore and distract strategy:

> **Child:** *"This is a mean horse. He's going to bite your nose off."*
> **Parent:** [ignores and distracts] *"My cow is going to play nicely over here. He is showing all of the other animals how to play on the see-saw. There they go. . . up and down!"*
> **Child:** [begins building a fence]
> **Parent:** [returns attention to the child] *"I'm glad you're playing gently again so I can play with you. You're building a fence for the animals. That's nice of you to make a home for them."*

When a parent ignores a child's negative attention-seeking behavior, the natural result is an escalation of the misbehavior. Because a less annoying version of the behavior is not getting the desired effect, children will try a more disruptive version to obtain parental attention. For ignoring to be effective, parents must ignore until the child engages in a neutral or positive behavior. As mentioned above, parental use of distraction (i.e., enthusiastically describing their own play) can minimize the escalation. In addition, the ignoring rules are explained and modeled for the child before special playtime begins (see section on "logistical issues" later in this chapter) so they recognize ignoring faster and can self-correct more quickly. Occasionally, however, a child may escalate from a minor disruptive behavior to a dangerous or destructive behavior. In such cases, the parent is to respond to the dangerous behavior by ending the special playtime (For more information on strategic ignoring, see Chapter Four).

Selecting Toys

Special playtime incorporates only those toys and activities that set children up for calm and prosocial behavior. Obviously, it is difficult to work on relationship building and self-esteem enhancement when children are aggressive, loud, frenetic, and destructive. Thus, there are several categories of toys which are excluded from special playtime. First, have parents avoid toys that tend to elicit aggressive themes, such as toy weapons, superhero figures, and toy soldiers. Second, toys that promote rough and tumble play, such as bats and balls, are excluded. Materials that can cause a mess or lead to destruction of property also may be excluded for certain children. These include paints, scissors, glue, and clay. The rationale for avoiding messy toys is that it is difficult to let the child lead the play and to remain positive when children are making a mess. Structured activities, such as board games, are discouraged because of their emphasis on competition. Finally, although we strongly encourage parents to read books to their children during other times of the day, we discourage the use of books during special playtime because they do not provide many opportunities for interactive conversation and praise of the child's accomplishments.

The best materials for special playtime are construction-oriented toys that encourage creativity and imagination. Because these toys have no rules and no "right" or "wrong" ways to play, they set children up for positive experiences. The child has an opportunity to be praised for good ideas and small accomplishments. Additionally, the creative nature of the play encourages communication of thoughts and feelings, and the hands-on activities allow the parent to imitate the child's play. Examples of appropriate toys for special playtime include farm sets, building blocks, magnetic figures, kitchen sets, crayons and paper, and play garages. See the Appendix for a parent handout that provides additional information regarding toy selection.

Logistical Issues

To start special playtime, parents select three or four acceptable toys or activities and place them in a space free of distractors. Children are not given the option of selecting the toys themselves because they may choose inappropriate activities, setting the stage for power struggles. We advise parents to avoid rooms containing competing activities such as television, toys that are attractive but unacceptable for special playtime, and rambunctious pets and siblings. Parents are asked to avoid answering the telephone during special playtime. The ideal setting is a quiet area where the parent and child will not be interrupted (e.g., a guest bedroom, formal dining room, a patio table).

After the toys have been selected, the parent tells the child that it is time for special playtime and the rules are explained as follows:

This is our special playtime. You can play with any of these toys in front of us, and I'll play along with you. There are two rules. First, you have to stay right here with me. And second, you have to play gently with the toys. If you wander around the room or play roughly with the toys, I will turn around like this and play by myself. Then, when you come back or play nicely again, I'll turn back around like this and play with you again. Thanks for listening to the rules. We can play with anything you want to play with now.

We encourage parents to restrict special playtime to five to ten minutes. Rather than setting a timer which could cause playtime to end abruptly, we recommend that parents look for a natural stopping point after approximately five minutes. That means the playtime could stretch up to 10 minutes to allow a child to complete a construction activity like building a tower.

Some disruptive children have difficulty ending special playtime. Offering a transition statement approximately one minute before playtime is over helps some children to prepare themselves to end. Others respond negatively to a transition statement by becoming anxious and distracted as they worry about the limited amount of time remaining. Another strategy for helping disruptive children end their playtime is to routinely schedule it so that it precedes another desirable activity (e.g., dessert, a favorite TV program, reading a story). For children who are intensely focused on a playtime activity, parents may choose to allow them to continue playing independently while the parent disengages from the play. We encourage parents to conclude the playtime by offering some labeled praise for what they have enjoyed about the play. They might summarize the positive aspects of the play by saying something like, "It's time for special playtime to be over now. I had a great time playing with you today. I especially liked the way you set up the corral for the sheep and showed me how to feed them. You were very kind to the animals. And you built a really cool barn for them to sleep in. Now it's time for clean up."

Because disruptive children are often reluctant to clean up the toys after special playtime, parents should be taught a strategy to enlist cooperation. Because the playtime should not end on a negative and critical note, we advise parents not to give clean-up directions. Instead, skills are used to entice children to volunteer to assist in putting toys away. Many children will respond favorably to parental modeling of clean up accompanied by enthusiastic and creative descriptions of the activity. The first time the child shows any inclination to help clean up the toys, the parent should provide animated labeled praise. For example:

Parent: *"I'm going to pick up the toys now. You can help if you want to. I'm going to pretend like these blocks are spaceships and the bucket is the moon. Here goes a handful of spaceships to the moon!"*
Child: *"I've got some spaceships. I'll fly them to the moon."*
Parent: *"Thanks for helping me pick up the toys. It's fun when we clean up together. I'm putting the people back in the house. It's time for them to sleep."*
Child: [puts pieces in the house]
Parent: *"You're being a terrific helper!"*

Should a child choose not to help clean up the toys, the parent should clean up the toys alone and ignore the lack of cooperation. We explain to parents that there are many other opportunities throughout the day to teach children to clean up toys. This is not an objective of special playtime. It is preferable for parents to avoid a struggle at the end of playtime by simply picking the toys up independently.

A difficult logistical issue for busy families is how to fit the playtime into a tight schedule. We problem-solve with families about possible times for special playtime. It is ideal for the playtime to occur at the same time every day. This type of routine is good for children. They are less likely to bother parents throughout the day with frequent requests for playtime, and parents are less likely to forget the playtime when it is part of their regular schedules. Possible times for parents to conduct playtime include: (a) immediately after bath/pajamas and before the bedtime story, (b) while a younger sibling is napping, (c) upon returning home from school and before an afternoon snack, and (d) after breakfast.

When there are one or more siblings between the ages of 2 and 12, we recommend that parents have special playtime with them as well (For older children, parents may substitute other developmentally appropriate forms of one-on-one time). For two-parent families with two children, it may be possible for each parent to play with a child for five minutes and then to switch partners. In other cases, parents may be able to stagger the playtime (e.g., have play-time with each child sequentially, have playtime with an older child while a younger child is napping, play with a younger child while an older child is at school). Therapists should save time at the end of the play therapy teaching session to problem-solve these types of scheduling issues with parents.

Role-Play

After all special playtime skills have been discussed and modeled for parents, role-play is con-ducted to allow for skill practice. When two parents are present, one parent can pretend to be the child while the other practices the skills. The therapist coaches as each parent takes a turn practicing the skills. For single-parent families, the therapist plays the role of the child and coaches the parent at the same time. In the beginning, the "child" is instructed to be very well-behaved so that the parent can gain some mastery and confidence. Later, the "child" can engage in some minor disruptive behavior so that the parent can practice ignoring. See Chapter Eight for information about how to coach parents during role-play.

Homework

Parents are given a homework assignment to spend 5 to 10 minutes of special playtime with their children on a daily basis. The therapist cautions that special playtime may not go smoothly at first. Because there has not yet been an opportunity to coach the parents in the skills as they interact with their child, it is possible that the child may not enjoy the playtime or may be disruptive during playtime. It also is possible that the parents may have difficulty implementing the skills. These problems are normalized for parents so that they do not become frustrated during their initial efforts at play therapy. The importance of doing the homework every day is stressed, particularly when the child has had a "bad" day. Parents may be tempted to withhold special playtime when their children engage in high rates of mis-behavior. We explain to them that children actually need more, rather than less, special play-time when they have displayed problematic behavior. Instead of withholding the sessions on those days, parents should consider extending the length of the playtime or making time for a second playtime. To help structure parents to do playtime each day, they are given a Special Playtime Homework Sheet (see Appendix) to complete and return the following session.

8

COACHING PARENTS IN PLAY THERAPY SKILLS: SESSIONS NINE THROUGH ELEVEN

The primary focus of Sessions Nine through Eleven is the direct coaching of play therapy skills as parents interact with their children. In more didactic approaches, the parents are taught a skill and sent home to practice it with their children throughout the week. Using the didactic method, parents of disruptive children often will return the following week with descriptions of failed attempts to implement the skills. In contrast, direct coaching offers the advantage of allowing therapists to problem-solve with parents as the problematic behaviors are occurring in the session.

The direct coaching method is more efficient than purely didactic approaches. Problems can be addressed immediately in the session, rather than losing an entire week of progress as parents become frustrated and discontinue skills practice. Direct coaching is one of the most expedient ways of acquiring new skills because it involves the use of two powerful learning strategies: rehearsal and immediate feedback. For added effectiveness, the direct coaching portion of our short-term treatment approach takes advantage of the principle of overlearning. Parents are coached to use skills at a high frequency (e.g., one statement of praise every 20 seconds) and with great precision. The overlearning of skills enhances generalization to other times and settings. The skills become such an ingrained part of the parenting repertoire that parents spontaneously and reflexively use them both in and out of special playtime.

Direct coaching of parents can take place either in the room or from behind a one-way mirror using a bug-in-the-ear approach. There are several advantages to coaching from behind a one-way mirror. First, the interaction between the parent and child is more natural and representative of their relationship at home when the therapist is out of the room. For example, children are more likely to test limits and engage in disruptive behavior when the therapist is not present. It is helpful for children to display some challenging behaviors in session so that the therapist can coach the parent to deal successfully with the problems. A second reason for coaching from behind a one-way mirror is that it gives parents the strong message that they will be the agent of change in this part of therapy. After all, the therapist is not even in the room. Being out of the room also allows for greater focus to be placed on skill practice. During in-room coaching, there is a tendency for the parents to stop playing and begin talking with the therapist about extraneous issues. A third advantage of out-of-room coaching is that it enables the therapist to give sensitive feedback to parents without the child hearing. A disadvantage of out-of-room coaching is that it requires a one-way mirror and special equipment. Many therapists simply do not have the resources to coach from outside the room.

Coaching from outside the room requires a one-way mirror, an intercom speaker system, and a bug-in-the-ear auditory transmission system. With the one-way mirror and speaker system, the therapist can see and hear the parent-child interaction, but the family is unable to see the therapist. The bug-in-the-ear system allows the therapist to talk to parents from behind the one-way mirror. The best available coaching system uses an unobtrusive, wireless, hearing-aid device. (This system is available from Mind Works, Inc., previously Farrall Instruments, 2701 Sea Lark Lane, Avalon Beach, Florida 32583-5611, PH: 1-904-995-5090, FAX: 1-904-994-3584.) Less-expensive versions can be obtained from national electronic stores, such as Radio Shack. These systems are more obtrusive in that they require that the parent wear a clip-on receiving box with a wire running from the box to the hearing aid. Inexpensive speaker systems also can be purchased from electronic stores, with some therapists electing to use simple baby monitors to transmit sound from the playroom to the observation room.

When coaching in the room, it is important that the therapist review some ground rules with the parent and child. Once the skill practice begins, all conversations between the therapist and parent should be postponed until the Check-Out period. Interactions between therapist and parent will be restricted to the coaching of skills. Similarly, it is important that the therapist not attend to the child at all during coaching. The child is told to pretend that the therapist is invisible and to ignore the therapist's coaching. The therapist cannot talk directly to the child during coaching because valuable parent-child interactional time can be lost as the child attempts to gain the therapist's attention. When coaching in the room, the therapist is positioned to the side and slightly behind the parent, on the side away from the child. The therapist should be positioned close enough to the parent to give feedback in a soft voice and an inconspicuous manner.

Whether coaching in or out of the room, therapists should remain cognizant of the great degree of performance anxiety that parents may experience while being coached. It is threatening to have a mental health professional provide feedback about parenting style. Parents feel very emotional and sensitive about their parenting abilities and can easily feel criticized or judged when given suggestions for improvement. Thus, coaching must always be conducted in a positive and gentle fashion, always balancing the need to obtain skill improvement expediently with the need to maintain a healthy rapport with parents. For more information about the subtleties of coaching play therapy skills, please see Hembree-Kigin and McNeil (1995).

Methods of Coaching

Give Feedback After Each Verbalization. Coaching is most effective when feedback is provided consistently after each parental verbalization. With this approach, the maximum degree of productivity is gained from the limited coaching period. Skills are constantly being shaped through prompting and reinforcement. When coaching is provided sporadically, there are many missed opportunities for skill development. Additionally, it can be confusing to parents when coaches are inconsistent in providing feedback. Parents do not know when to pause to listen to the therapist, so the therapist often ends up "talking over" the parent. When feedback is given after each verbalization, the therapist and parent can develop a cadence in which the parent learns to always pause and listen to feedback before providing the next comment. This type of coaching requires that the therapist be alert and active. Therapists must fight the tendency to simply sit back and watch the special playtime. It is the continuous and active coaching that leads to quick and meaningful improvements in play therapy skills.

Emphasize the Positive. Recognizing that parents are anxious about their performance and sensitive to criticism, it is important to remain positive while coaching. Rather than pointing out what parents are doing wrong, therapists should tell them what to do instead. Table 8-1 provides examples of critical and more constructive coaching. One way to maintain a positive coaching atmosphere is to include frequent labeled praise. Parents can be praised for good use of the "do" skills, as well as for nonspecific factors (e.g., being warm and genuine, being playful). See Table 8-2 for a listing of labeled praise that can be used during coaching. Additionally, humor can be included in the coaching to promote a more relaxed atmosphere, as long as it will not be perceived by the parent as offensive or sarcastic. Tension in the coaching session can be lessened when the therapist laughs with the family when humorous events occur (e.g., the child tells a joke, the parent and child create a silly alien, the child sings a funny song).

Table 8-1. Critical Versus Constructive Coaching

Avoid Critical Coaching	Focus on Constructive Coaching
Parent: *"What are you making?"* **Therapist:** *"Don't ask questions."*	**Parent:** *"What are you making?"* **Therapist:** *"Say, you are making a circle."* **Parent:** *"You are making a circle."* **Therapist:** *"Good job of saying that as a statement. There was no question in your voice that time."*
Parent: *"Hand me a block."* **Therapist:** *"Remember, no directions."*	
Parent: *"Don't write on the table!"* **Therapist:** *"I don't want you to criticize."*	**Parent:** *"Hand me a block."* **Therapist:** *"Just reach over and grab a block. Good job of keeping him in the lead."*
	Parent: *"Don't write on the table!"* **Therapist:** *"Turn and ignore that. Great job of ignoring. Now model for him how you can color on the paper. Say, I'm drawing a pretty picture on the paper. He's coloring on the paper now. Turn back around and give him a big praise statement. Terrific job with that ignoring."*

Table 8-2. Common Behavioral Play Therapy Coaching Statements

LABELED PRAISE
Good imitation.
Nice eye-contact.
Great teaching!
I like how you're ignoring now.
Nice physical praise.
Terrific enthusiasm!
Great job following his lead.
Good description.
Nice labeled praise.
Good encouraging his creativity.
Good answering his question.
Nice timing on giving him back your attention.

GENTLE CORRECTIONS
Oops, a question!
A little leading.
Was that a command?
Looks like a frown.
Sounds a little critical.
Might be better to say. . .
You're getting a little ahead of her now.

DIRECTIVES
Try to label it.
What can you praise now?
Can you reflect that?
Say, "Nice manners!"
Praise her for sharing.
More enthusiasm!
Say it again, but drop your voice at the end.
Say, "I like it when you use your big girl voice."
Let's ignore until he does something neutral or positive.
Say, "It's so much fun to play with you when you're careful with the toys."
How about a hug with that praise?

OBSERVATIONS
He's enjoying this.
Sounds very genuine.
He's sitting nicely now.
Now he's imitating you.
She wants to please you.
He loves that praise.
He's talking more now because you're reflecting.
She's staying with it longer because of your descriptions.
That praise is good for her self-esteem.
That's good practice for fine motor skills.

She's handling frustration a little better now.
There's a big self-esteem smile!
You see, anything you praise will increase.
By saying "I'm sorry" you just set a good example for polite manners.

From Hembree-Kigin & McNeil (1995). *Parent-Child Interaction Therapy.* New York: Plenum Publishing Corporation.
Reprinted by permission.

Use Brief, Specific Feedback. Although an occasional, lengthy observation may be provided to parents, the majority of coaching consists of brief, specific phrases. This type of coaching requires therapists to become comfortable with new terminology and abbreviated methods of communicating to parents. Much of the basic coaching involves combining a praise word with the name of the skill that the parent has employed. Examples include, "Good describing," "Nice labeled praise," "Excellent ignoring," and "Great reflection." Concise instructions also can be given to parents with such phrases as, "Ignore that," "Say...," "Praise her for sharing," "Go ahead and describe that," "Try to reflect her speech." See Table 8-2 for additional examples of brief directives that can be used during coaching.

Be Selective When Correcting Repetitive Mistakes. There will be times when parents make numerous errors, particularly when first being coached. Providing frequent suggestions for improvement can promote a tense atmosphere in which the parent feels pressured to perform better. One option for maintaining good rapport and a positive atmosphere is to ignore some of the errors. In this case, the general rule of coaching after each verbalization can be temporarily suspended. Rather than overwhelming the parent with many suggestions and corrections, the therapist can ignore repetitive errors selectively. As soon as the parent produces an appropriate play therapy skill, the therapist can provide an enthusiastic labeled praise statement. An example of this coaching method is described below:

> **Parent:** [asks a question] *"What is your puppet's name?"*
> **Therapist:** [ignores]
> **Parent:** [asks another question] *"Is her name Sarah?"*
> **Therapist:** [ignores]
> **Parent:** [describes] *"Your puppet is putting on a hat."*
> **Therapist:** *"Great description! You said that as a definitive statement. There was no question there at all."*

Coach Qualitative Aspects of the Parent-Child Interaction. Once the parents have begun to gain some proficiency in the "do" and "don't" skills of play therapy, the therapist begins to coach more qualitative aspects of the parent-child interaction. In addition to the basic skills, good play therapy involves a number of more subtle features, such as enthusiasm, eye contact, smiles, physical closeness, expression of feelings, patience, playfulness, and creativity. The therapist should be aware of these qualitative features, prompting and encouraging them whenever possible. Additionally, once basic behavioral goals for the child have been achieved (e.g., playing gently, staying in the room), the therapist can coach the parent to address specific issues. For example, contingent attention can be used to encourage polite manners, planning ahead, sharing, trying difficult tasks, turn-taking, handling frustration, and using words to express feelings. The following example illustrates how coaching can be used to address more complex and qualitative interactions:

Child: *"Oh no. My tower fell over! I'm gonna build it again."*

Therapist: *"How about giving him a praise for effort?"*

Father: *"I'm proud of you for starting over. You didn't get upset and quit. You kept a positive attitude."*

Therapist: *"Great, specific praise. You'll see more trying now."*

Child: *"I was mad when it fell down. I felt like screaming but I didn't."*

Therapist: *"Say, 'I like it when you use your words to talk about how you feel instead of screaming.'"*

Be Decisive, Directive, and Quick When Coaching Ignoring. When a child engages in a negative attention-seeking behavior, the therapist has only seconds to coach the parent to ignore. Otherwise, the parent is likely to react to the misbehavior, thereby rewarding it. Therefore, therapists must make a quick decision regarding whether the behavior is appropriate or inappropriate. If the behavior is inappropriate, the therapist should provide a firm directive for the parent to turn, ignore, and distract. To save time and ensure that parents respond effectively, it is best to provide parents with very specific directions. Consider the following example:

Child: [throws truck against the wall]

Therapist: *"Ignore that. Turn away quickly. Good ignoring. Now describe your own play with lots of enthusiasm."*

Child: [brings truck back to parent] *"Do you want to play with the truck?"*

Therapist: *"Turn back around and say, 'Thanks for sharing the truck with me. I am glad that you are playing gently now so we can play together.'"*

Evaluating Skill Acquisition

Parental acquisition of play therapy skills is evaluated using a coding sheet (see Appendix). Parental use of "do" and "don't" skills is recorded continuously during a five-minute coding period. This coding period occurs after Check-In and before the coaching begins. To get an accurate appraisal of how well parents do the play therapy skills on their own, it is important that coding take place prior to coaching. When coding takes place immediately after coaching, the high level of skill performance usually obtained is more likely due to the short-term effects of coaching and may not be indicative of parental ability to perform the skills independently at home. Before coding, parents are asked to demonstrate their best play therapy skills during the five-minute recording period. The therapist uses the coding data to guide the focus of coaching (e.g., more emphasis on changing unlabeled praise to labeled praise). During Check-Out, the therapist provides feedback to the parent on skill progress. The parent's performance in one session can be compared to previous sessions. Additionally, the parent can be given some goals to strive for. Sample goals for the frequency of "do" and "don't" skills during a five-minute coding period are listed in Table 8-3.

Table 8-3. Skill Acquisition Objectives

Skill	Objective
Descriptions	25
Reflections	10 - 15 (For children who do not talk much during the five-minute period, the goal is to reflect nearly all appropriate verbalizations)
Imitation	Continuously follow child's choice of activity when child is playing appropriately
Praise	15 (at least 8 of which are labeled praises)
Directions	0
Questions	0
Criticisms	0
Ignore	Ignore all negative attention-seeking behaviors

Coaching Two-Parent Families

When two caregivers are involved in therapy, each will be coached individually with the child. The coaching time is divided in half. In the first half, one of the parents will be coached while the other observes. In the second half, the parents switch roles. By having parents observe when not being coached, learning occurs through modeling as well as direct coaching. For out-of-room coaching, the observing parent watches from behind the one-way mirror. For in-room coaching, the observing parent sits in a corner of the room, far from the interaction. The observing parent is told to remain quiet during the coaching, and to refrain from interacting with the child. Each parent is coded separately during the first five minutes of their coaching time.

Structuring Sessions Nine Through Eleven

Sessions Nine through Eleven begin with a Check-In period. During this time, the previous homework assignment is reviewed, including daily special playtime and remaining Child's Work assignments. Before the coaching begins, there is a 5-minute coding period to assess parental progress toward skill acquisition goals. Then, parents are coached in the use of play therapy skills. After the coaching is completed, the parent leaves so that the therapist can spend individual time with the child in both Child's Work and Child's Play. To maintain the previously-set precedent, children are given a brief bathroom and drink break prior to their individual time with the therapist. In preparation for termination, the amount of time devoted to individual work with the child is gradually diminished over Sessions Nine through Eleven.

The last few minutes of each session are devoted to Check-Out with the parent and child. During this time, the results of the coding are shared with parents, and they receive specific feedback about progress and the skills that need additional work. They are told to continue daily special playtime sessions and may be given additional Child's Work homework assignments (e.g., relaxation practice).

Session Nine. With one parent, time in this session is allocated as follows: Check-In (10 minutes), coding of skills (5 minutes), coaching (20 minutes), Child's Work/Child's Play (15 minutes), and Check-Out (10 minutes). With two parents, the time allocation is Check-In (10 minutes), coding of first parent (5 minutes), coaching of first parent (10 minutes), coding of second parent (5 minutes), coaching of second parent (10 minutes), Child's Work/Child's Play (15 minutes), and Check-Out (10 minutes). To emphasize the importance of daily special playtime, the session begins with a review of the parent's Special Playtime Homework Sheet. The therapist should help parents feel accountable for home practice by a detailed, day-by-day examination of the play sessions. In the case of missed play sessions, therapists prompt parents to problem-solve about how they can avoid missing special playtime during the upcoming week. When parents fail to bring in their homework sheets, we ask them to reconstruct the sheets with the therapist, reinforcing the point that homework is a priority. As this is the first play therapy coaching session, part of the Check-in time is spent in an overview of the new session structure for parents and children. The child is reminded that the therapist will still spend some individual time with him or her. When coaching is conducted from within the playroom, children are prepared for the coaching as follows:

> In a couple of minutes, you and your mom will get to have some special playtime like you have been having at home. While you and your mom are playing, my job is to watch you and teach your mom some special ways of playing with you. Sometimes, I'll say some silly things to your mom, like "nice praise" and "Can you reflect that?" Your job is to play and have fun. I want you to pretend like I am the invisible man [woman], like you can't see me and you can't hear me, like I'm not even here. There is a rule that if you talk to me, I can't answer you. We'll get a chance to talk to each other later. Thanks for being such a good listener.

Immediately prior to coding, parents are told to review with their child the special playtime rules (e.g., the child must stay in the playroom, parents will turn and ignore disruptive play) and to do their very best job of play therapy while the therapist codes their skills. After five minutes of coding, the therapist begins coaching the "do" skills. In this first coaching session, emphasis usually is placed on the two easiest skills for parents to master: description and imitation. To assist parents in describing, the therapist might say, "Just talk about what his hands are doing." Parents can be prompted to imitate by saying, "He's building. Can you do that too?" As parents are particularly sensitive to criticism during the first coaching session, therapists should provide many more praises than gentle corrections.

During individual time with the therapist, the child's thoughts and feelings about the coaching session are processed. Children are encouraged to talk with the therapist about the following: (a) what they think about their special playtime sessions at home, (b) how "funny" it is to have the therapist watching them play and coaching their parents, and (c) how they feel about spending less individual time with the therapist. To help children assimilate the impending termination of treatment, a termination ritual is introduced. For example, the therapist and child may draw a picture of a staircase with each stair representing one of the remaining treatment sessions, the Staircase to Termination (see Appendix). At the top of the stairs, there could be a picture depicting the end-of-treatment party. The therapist and child can spend time in each of the remaining sessions referring back to the staircase. A marker can be moved up the steps to help the child visualize the number of sessions remaining. After the Child's Work addressing termination issues, several minutes are spent in child-directed play. The last 10 minutes are spent debriefing the parents on their skill progress (using data generated during coding) and assigning the parents to implement daily play therapy sessions at home.

Session Ten. With one parent, time in this session is allocated as follows: Check-In (10 minutes), coding of skills (5 minutes), coaching (25 minutes), Child's Work/Child's Play (10 minutes), and Check-Out (10 minutes). With two parents, the time allocation is similar except that the coding and coaching time is divided between the two parents. During Check-In, a great deal of emphasis is again placed on the importance of providing daily special play-time. Coaching in this session is focused on decreasing questions and increasing two of the more difficult skills, labeled praise and reflection. To reduce questions, the therapist selectively attends to comments that are stated definitively. The therapist uses feedback such as, "Good describing. You said that with no question in your voice," and "Nice reflection. You repeated that with certainty." The following examples demonstrate how to prompt parents to turn unlabeled praise into labeled praise:

Example 1.
Parent: *"That's nice."*
Therapist: *"What's nice?"*
Parent: *"That's nice the way that you picked up the toy that fell on the ground."*
Therapist: *"Excellent labeled praise. We can expect him to pick up fallen objects more*
often because you praised it."

Example 2.
Parent: *"Thank you."*
Therapist: *"Thanks for what?"*
Parent: *"Thanks for helping me hold the tower."*
Therapist: *"Good job of labeling that praise."*

Example 3.
Parent: *"I like that."*
Therapist: *"Try to be more specific with your praise."*
Parent: *"I like the blue dinosaur that you made."*
Therapist: *"Great labeled praise. That's good for his self-esteem."*

For increasing skills like labeled praise and reflection, exercises often are used in this session. The therapist tells parents that it is time to try a special exercise. The parent is to try to reflect every appropriate verbalization made by the child within a two-minute period. Once the timing has begun, the therapist counts each reflection aloud by saying, "Good, there's one reflection. . . There's two. . . Keep going. . . There's three." Similarly the parent can be asked to give as much labeled praise as possible in the next two minutes, and the therapist counts each instance. Immediately following the exercise, feedback is given to parents about their progress toward skill goals. These exercises are beneficial in that they allow the parents to improve skill deficiencies by concentrating on one skill at a time.

Following the coaching, the therapist spends approximately 10 minutes in individual time with the child. Again, the number of remaining sessions is reviewed with the child (e.g., by examining the Staircase to Termination that depicts the movement toward termination). Some time also is spent in child-directed play. In Check-Out, the results of the coding are shared with parents. A homework assignment is given to continue 5 to 10 minutes of daily special playtime.

Session Eleven. Post-treatment evaluation is conducted in Session Eleven to provide parents with feedback on pre- to post-treatment changes during Session Twelve. This information also is used to provide feedback to third-party reimbursors. Because extra time is needed to conduct the post-treatment evaluation procedures, Session Eleven is expanded to 90 minutes. Time in this session is allocated as follows: Check-In (10 minutes), completion of post-treatment evaluation measures (30 minutes), coding of skills (5 minutes with one parent, 10 minutes with two parents), coaching (20 minutes), Child's Work/Child's Play (15 minutes), and Check-Out (10 minutes). Following Check-In, all pretreatment measures are repeated. The parent completes rating scales (e.g., CBCL) while the therapist re-administers child-report measures (e.g., Children's Depression Inventory). Any teacher report inventories are given to the parent to deliver to the teacher. Parents are asked to bring the teacher report form to the termination session.

Following the five minutes of coding, parents are coached in play therapy skills. As this is the final coaching session, emphasis is placed on motivating parents to continue providing special playtime on a daily basis long after therapy is terminated. This is accomplished by reinforcing the parents' sense of competence and mastery of skills. Additionally, parents are more motivated to continue daily practice when therapists point out the therapeutic benefits that can be attributed to their hard work. For example, if a child says, "I've got a great idea!" the therapist might observe aloud, "That's a sign of high self-esteem. Your praise is really paying off." Should a child spontaneously offer a toy to his father, the therapist can say, "He's sharing so much more than he used to. You've taught him to do that with your modeling and your praise." Other observations can be provided to demonstrate the positive impact of special playtime on the warmth of the parent-child relationship and the child's (a) ability to handle frustration, (b) polite manners, (c) attention span, (d) calm and productive play, and (e) expression of feelings.

Individual time spent with the child again focuses on termination issues. The staircase towards termination is examined, with emphasis on the party that will occur next session. The therapist gathers ideas from the child regarding fun activities that can be included in the termination party. The child receives a great deal of labeled praise for his or her hard work in therapy and notable accomplishments. Then, a few minutes are devoted to child-directed play. In Check-Out, the coding sheets are again reviewed, and the therapist focuses on the parent's skill improvement. Parents are told that for maintenance of behavioral gains and continued child improvement they must continue the daily special playtime after the completion of therapy.

9

TERMINATING TREATMENT: SESSION TWELVE

In a short-term play therapy approach, there likely are fewer termination issues for children than in a longer-term intervention. After all, the child works with the therapist over a much shorter time-frame, and presumably becomes less attached. In our short-term play therapy, we specifically promote less attachment to the therapist, particularly toward the end of treatment. The therapist meets with the child for increasingly shorter periods of time and is spending more of the session time interacting with parents.

Although there may be fewer termination issues for children in short-term play therapy, our approach results in more termination issues for their parents. In long-term play therapy, the therapist and parent may not develop a strong attachment or dependence. However, in our short-term play therapy approach, we spend a significant amount of time with parents during the last third of treatment. A therapeutic relationship clearly develops as parents are taught new skills and receive a great deal of positive feedback from the therapist. Moreover, in our short-term play therapy model, only a small set of potential treatment goals are addressed. Parents may leave treatment recognizing progress yet wishing there were time to address additional goals. Recognition that there are things left undone makes it difficult for parents to obtain a sense of closure.

Several steps are taken prior to this last session to prepare families for termination (see Table 9-1). In the first session, a short-term play therapy contract is signed by the parent, indicating that therapy will be terminated after 12 sessions. Also during this first session, the time-limited nature of treatment is explained to the child. A significant portion of the seventh session is devoted to discussing termination with the child using *A Child's First Book About Play Therapy*. Parents also learn more about termination through a homework assignment that involves reading the termination section of this book to the child. Also, time is spent in each of the final sessions helping the child to understand the number of sessions remaining. We often use the Staircase to Termination handout (available in the Appendix) to help children visualize the remaining time. We have the child place a sticker (or draw a picture) on the step representing that particular session. As the sessions go by, the child associates the movement up the stairs with the progression of therapy. Both the staircase and therapy end with the end-of-treatment party.

By increasing parent involvement through coaching in Sessions Eight through Eleven, the child's dependence on the therapist is gradually diminished. The therapist spends increasingly less individual time with the child toward the end of treatment. In Session Eleven, the parents and child complete post-treatment measures related to presenting problems, and the child and the therapist plan the final session termination party. Toward the end of treatment, parents commonly express anxiety about termination and ask if they can have additional sessions. Whenever possible, we do recommend "booster" or follow-up sessions to maintain treatment gains and assist families in dealing with termination issues.

In the termination session, we maintain our basic structure but distribute time differently:

Table 9-1. Preparing Families for Termination

Session	Method
1	Establish therapy contract that emphasizes termination after 12 sessions
7	Present termination themes using *A Child's First Book About Play Therapy* Use a visual representation (e.g., "Staircase to Termination" in Appendix) to help child understand the number of sessions remaining
8 - 11	Gradually diminish individual time with child while devoting more time to enhancing the parent-child relationship
11	Parent and child complete post-treatment assessment forms Therapist and child plan termination celebration
12	Conduct termination rituals with parent: review treatment plan, examine pre- to post-treatment changes on measures, and praise parental accomplishments Conduct termination rituals with child: review course of treatment and have a post-treatment party
Follow-up	Schedule one or two "booster sessions" to address a few unresolved issues and gradually reduce dependence on the therapist

Check-In (20 minutes), Child's Work (10 minutes), Child's Play (20 minutes), and Check-Out (10 minutes). We use the Check-In time to accomplish important termination rituals with the parents. First, we give parents a copy of the treatment plan and review it with them in detail, emphasizing work completed. It often is difficult for families to remember early goals and accomplishments. There is a tendency to focus on the most recent sessions. Reviewing the treatment plan gives families an appreciation for the entire course of therapy.

The second termination ritual for parents during Check-In is the examination of pre- to post-treatment changes on outcome measures. This process helps them to value therapy accomplishments, while also highlighting areas of continued need. Parents are reminded that the purpose of short-term therapy is to give them and their child the tools needed to begin the change process. With these tools, families should be able to build on their successes with continued improvements long after termination. In some cases, the post-treatment evaluation reveals clinically significant concerns that warrant additional treatment. The data can be used to appeal for reimbursement of additional sessions or as grounds for making a referral to another professional.

A third termination ritual for parents during the Check-In period is to provide clear recognition of parental accomplishments. The parents receive specific praises for such achievements as recognizing the need for treatment, adhering to the Attendance Contract, completing homework assignments, and learning valuable "play therapy" skills. This positive feedback is designed to bolster the parents' sense of competence and to encourage their continued use of new skills.

The Child's Work portion of the last session is devoted to reviewing the course of play therapy with the child. Like their parents, children tend to forget the activities and accomplishments of early sessions. Just as the written treatment plan helps parents recall these details, an examination of therapy games and exercises helps children visualize the course of treatment and remember critical incidents. All treatment tools are displayed in the playroom, and the therapist goes through them one-by-one, reminiscing with the child about themes and skills. For example, the therapist might say:

> Remember when we played the "Talking, Feeling, and Doing Game?" You told me about the time that Carrie called your father a drunk. You thought about hitting Carrie, but you didn't. Do you remember what you did instead? Well, you used your words and told Carrie that was none of her business and she hurt your feelings. I'm glad you used your words instead of hitting, and I was very happy that you told me about what happened.

Examining the therapy tools reinforces the skills that the child has learned, while also instilling a sense of accomplishment.

Child's Play is devoted to a fun termination ritual. The exact nature of the ritual is determined in part by the child in Session Eleven. Typically, we celebrate the end of treatment with a termination party. This involves sharing a treat, giving the child a small gift (e.g., certificate of achievement, blue ribbon), and exchanging cards that are made in the session. After some individual time with the therapist, the child is given the option to include the parent(s) in the party. A brief Check-Out is included to say formal goodbyes to all family members.

10

CASE EXAMPLE: "JEREMY"

To illustrate how short-term play therapy may be used with a child with disruptive behavior problems, we will present a detailed case example. In Chapter One, we described a child named "Jeremy" who presented a number of challenges to his nondirective play therapist. Because of difficulty managing Jeremy's behavior, the therapist referred him for a more directive intervention. After describing Jeremy's presenting problems and the results of his intake evaluation, we will demonstrate the integration of short-term play therapy skills over the full course of treatment. In a session-by-session format, we will discuss the selection of treatment goals, formulation of session objectives, and incorporation of Child's Work and homework activities to address session objectives. As treatment unfolds, we will illustrate the use of play therapy process skills (particularly in Child's Play) and strategies for managing Jeremy's disruptive behavior.

Background Information

"Jeremy" is a seven-year-old boy with a three-year history of oppositional and aggressive behavior. He was referred for play therapy after the death of his 20-month-old sister, "Leslie." During the intake evaluation, the mother, "Ms. J.," reported that she had asked Jeremy to watch Leslie while they were playing in the back yard. The children were outside for approximately 10 minutes when Ms. J. looked out her kitchen window and saw Leslie lying on the ground having a seizure. There was a bottle of weed killer next to Leslie's hand. As Ms. J. rushed to Leslie's side, Jeremy ran over to a tire swing and began to swing. Ms. J. commented that Jeremy acted "as if he didn't care that his sister was hurt; like he just wanted to have fun. He didn't even try to get help."

Since his sister's death three months ago, Jeremy has continued residing with his mother, who is a single parent. Jeremy's father lives out of state and has not been in contact with Jeremy since he was two years old. Ms. J. reported a number of concerns about Jeremy's adjustment to his sister's death. First, Jeremy's behavior problems have escalated over the past three months, and he has become very difficult for his mother to control. She described an incident in which Jeremy attacked an older boy. Apparently, the older boy had provoked Jeremy by saying, "I heard you killed your sister." A second concern expressed by Ms. J. was Jeremy's decreased interest in playing with other children. She reported that he has become very quiet, talking little to others, and preferring to be alone. A third concern reported by Ms. J. was Jeremy's frequent nightmares. In an average week, Jeremy awakened crying twice during the night, crawling into his mother's bed with her. When asked about her own adjustment to Leslie's death, Ms. J. tearfully reported that she had been depressed and was receiving ongoing individual therapy.

Results of Pretreatment Measures

To assist in clarifying the severity and scope of Jeremy's presenting problems and to provide baseline measures of emotional and behavioral adjustment, the following parent-report rating scales were administered: the Eyberg Child Behavior Inventory (ECBI) and the Child Behavior Checklist/4-18 (CBCL). The items of the Children's Depression Inventory (CDI) were read to Jeremy, and the Harter Pictorial Scale of Perceived Competence and Social Acceptance for Young Children was administered. In addition, Jeremy's teacher completed the teacher-report version of the CBCL. Results of Jeremy's pretreatment evaluation are summarized in Table 10-1.

Results of the pretreatment evaluation indicate clinically significant problems in several areas. Jeremy's mother and teacher both produced clinically elevated ratings on the Anxious/Depressed Scale of the CBCL. On the Children's Depression Inventory, Jeremy received scores in the "much above average" range on the Negative Mood, Anhedonia, and Total Scales. Associated problems with self-esteem were evident on the Maternal and Peer Acceptance Scales of the Harter. These scores were consistent with Jeremy's above-average score on the Negative Self-esteem Scale of the CDI. Both Ms. J. and Jeremy's teacher endorsed items on the CBCL reflecting concerns regarding his peer interactional skills (i.e., elevated scores on the Social Problems and Withdrawn Scales). Ms. J.'s scores on both the ECBI and CBCL are consistent with significant behavior problems at home. However, Jeremy's teacher did not report an unusual number of behavior problems in the school setting.

The results of the intake evaluation were used, in combination with information gathered in Sessions One and Two, to formulate a treatment plan (see Table 10-2). In collaboration with Jeremy and Ms. J., the following three play therapy goals were identified: (a) reduced depression, (b) increased sociability, and (c) improved self-esteem. As part of the treatment plan, session objectives were outlined to ensure steady progress toward goals.

Table 10-1. Summary of Jeremy's Pretreatment Evaluation

Scale	Pre-Tx
Child Behavior Checklist (parent report)	
Internalizing	T = 77
Externalizing	T = 73
Withdrawn	T = 84
Somatic Complaints	T = 56
Anxious/Depressed	T = 81
Social Problems	T = 70
Thought Problems	T = 67
Attention Problems	T = 65
Delinquent Behavior	T = 63
Aggressive Behavior	T = 80
Sex Problems	T = 50
Eyberg Child Behavior Inventory	
Problem Score	20
Intensity Score	153

Table 10-1. (continued)

Children's Depression Inventory

Total CDI Raw Score	T = 67
Negative Mood	T = 70
Interpersonal Problems	T = 57
Ineffectiveness	T = 54
Anhedonia	T = 67
Negative Self-Esteem	T = 62

Harter

Cognitive Competence	3.67
Peer Acceptance	2.00
Physical Competence	3.83
Maternal Acceptance	1.33

Child Behavior Checklist (teacher report)

Internalizing	T = 75
Externalizing	T = 61
Withdrawn	T = 83
Somatic Complaints	T = 50
Anxious/Depressed	T = 71
Social Problems	T = 76
Thought Problems	T = 58
Attention Problems	T = 61
Delinquent Behavior	T = 50
Aggressive Behavior	T = 63

Session One

Session Objectives: (a) Obtain parental consent and child assent for treatment; (b) Agree on an attendance contract; (c) Introduce the parent and child to basic concepts about play therapy; (d) establish playroom rules and behavioral expectations; and (e) Build rapport.

Check-In. Although Jeremy stared at the floor and did not respond when the therapist introduced herself, he complied with his mother's request that he accompany her and the therapist to the Check-In room. Jeremy sat sullenly in a chair during the Check-In period, choosing neither to speak to the therapist nor play with available toys. His mother explained that he did not want to come to his appointment today, telling Ms. J. that he thought it was "dumb." Ms. J. read and signed the informed consent. Rather than request Jeremy's assent for treatment at this time, the therapist chose to wait until later in the session, after initial rapport had been established. The family was given an introduction to the nature of play therapy, including the structure of sessions and the importance of regular attendance. After Ms. J. signed the Attendance Contract, Jeremy was told that it was time to go see the playroom with the therapist. Jeremy looked down and seemed reluctant to leave. The therapist gently took Jeremy's hand and began guiding him to the playroom. On the way, she said, "I picked out some special toys that I thought you might like. First we have an interesting book to look at together. Then we get to play some fun games. Thanks for walking with me."

Child's Work. Jeremy was introduced to play therapy concepts using *A Child's First Book*

Table 10-2. Treatment Plan for Case Example

Child's Name: Jeremy J.   **Date:** July 15, 1995
Goal #1: Reduced depression
Goal #2: Increased sociability
Goal #3: Improved self-esteem

Session	Child's Work Activity	Homework Assignment
1	*A Child's First Book About Play Therapy* Practice listening skills Review playroom rules	Read play therapy book
2	Complete *A Child's First Book About Play Therapy* Review listening skills and playroom rules Exercise for labeling feelings	Continue reading play therapy book Practice labeling feelings
3	"Talking, Feeling, & Doing Game" Continue labeling feelings "Ups and Downs with Feelings" audiotape	Practice labeling feelings
4	*When Someone Very Special Dies* workbook	Go over workbook at home
5	*When Someone Very Special Dies* workbook Turtle technique for self-control	Go over workbook at home Prompt and reward use of turtle technique at home and school
6	Exercise for labeling feelings of guilt *My Best Friend Is Me!* book on self-esteem Self-esteem exercise	Read self-esteem book Conduct daily self-esteem exercise
7	Use special game rules to generate examples of guilt Guilt exercise on chalkboard Cognitive strategy for minimizing guilt Read termination section of play therapy book "Staircase to termination"	Read termination section of play therapy book
8	Teach mother play therapy skills (Jeremy is not present)	Practice "special playtime" for five minutes each day
9	Coach Ms. J. in play therapy skills as she interacts with Jeremy "Staircase to termination"	Practice "special playtime" for five minutes each day
10	Coach Ms. J. in play therapy skills as she interacts with Jeremy "Staircase to termination"	Practice "special playtime" for five minutes each day
11	Coach Ms. J. in play therapy skills as she interacts with Jeremy Repeat pre-treatment measures "Staircase to termination" Plan termination party	Practice "special playtime" for five minutes each day
12	Review Jeremy's progress toward goals Termination rituals (e.g., party)	Continue practicing "special playtime" on a daily basis

About Play Therapy. He paid attention to the pictures in the book and listened as the therapist read to him. When the therapist reached the section describing the kinds of problems that children have who go to play therapy, she asked Jeremy, "What problems do you have that we could work on in play therapy?" Jeremy responded by shrugging his shoulders and looking at the floor. The therapist told Jeremy, "Your mother already told me about a really big problem that your family has. Your little sister died from drinking weed killer in the backyard. Everyone in your family has important feelings about this. You don't have to talk to me about Leslie today, but sometime later in our play therapy we will talk a lot about her."

After reading the first third of the play therapy book, Jeremy's attention appeared to wane. The therapist marked her place in the book with a paper clip and took this opportunity to teach Jeremy how to be a good listener (i.e., "Look right in my eyes when I talk," "Hold your body very still like a statue," and "Think hard about what I am saying.") Jeremy received handstamps and dinosaur stickers as rewards for his good performance. Once listening skills were established, the playroom rules were explained to Jeremy. He looked away and fiddled with his shoe as the therapist explained the rules. He quickly returned his attention, however, upon being prompted and rewarded for using his good listening skills.

Child's Play. During Child's Play, Jeremy selected blocks and began building in the corner of the room, with his back turned to the therapist. The therapist selected another set of blocks and moved near Jeremy so that his building was in view. She used child-directed play therapy skills to describe and imitate his play. To encourage Jeremy to turn around and not exclude the therapist, the therapist described her own activity with enthusiasm. When Jeremy turned to view the "dune buggy" being constructed by the therapist, she said, "Thanks for turning around, Jeremy. Now I can see better what you're making. That's a cool pattern you put on your walls!" Jeremy turned around further and moved his structure closer to the therapist. As Child's Play progressed, he talked more and more to the therapist, occasionally making eye contact and commenting on aspects of their play. At five minutes before Child's Play was over, the therapist gave Jeremy the following transition warning: "In just a few minutes, it will be time to stop playing and clean up." When Child's Play was over, Jeremy was told about the therapist's clean-up rule. He was excited at the prospect of receiving a "good behavior prize" and cleaned up the playroom without protest. After selecting a good behavior prize, the therapist told Jeremy that she would like for them to tell his mother about the book they looked at together today and about the playroom rules. He agreed that this would be okay, and the therapist escorted Jeremy back to the Check-out room. He was clearly excited about showing his mother the matchbox car he had selected.

Check-Out. During Check-Out, the therapist spoke with the mother briefly about the content of Jeremy's first Child's Work session. Ms. J. was given an inexpensive paper copy of the book, *A Child's First Book About Play Therapy,* and for homework she was asked to read it with her son at least twice during the week. Ms. J. was instructed to read only up to the page marked by the therapist. The therapist elicited Jeremy's assistance in recounting for Ms. J. the playroom rules, rewarding him with praise and a handstamp for being a good listener and having a good memory. Because Jeremy's assent for treatment had not yet been obtained, the therapist took this opportunity to ask him if he would like to come back again next week to play with her. He enthusiastically agreed, surprising his mother. Jeremy signed the assent line of the treatment consent form.

Session Two

Session Objectives: (a) Introduce play therapy concepts not covered in Session One; (b) Reinforce playroom rules and behavioral expectations; (c) Practice using age-appropriate affective labels; and (d) Build rapport.

Check-In. Upon arriving for the second session, Jeremy greeted the therapist enthusiastically and began walking ahead to the playroom. The therapist responded by saying, "Jeremy, please come over here. I have something important to talk with you about." When Jeremy walked over, the therapist praised him for coming back right away. Then she said,

> Let's see those good listening skills. There you go! You're looking right in my eyes, and you're holding very still. Oops, I see your feet moving. There's that statue. Now, think very hard about what I am saying. When you come for play therapy, the first thing we do is walk to our Check-in room with your mom. The rule is that we all have to walk together. You did a great job of listening. I'm going to stamp your hand for that. Now, let's practice walking back together. Thanks for staying right with me.

During Check-in, Jeremy played with blocks while the therapist talked with his mother. Ms. J. immediately was asked about how the homework assignment went. She said that it had been a hectic week, and she had not had an opportunity to look at the play therapy book. Recognizing the need to establish a good homework precedent with the mother, the therapist responded by saying,

> I'm sorry that you did not get to the homework this week, but I appreciate you being honest with me about it. The homework is extremely important for the success of this treatment. We are trying to accomplish a lot in a short amount of time. It is the homework that makes it possible. How does next week look? What two days might be easiest to plan time to read the book? Can you commit to doing that next week? Good. What I will do today is try to review that material with him quickly. But I will still need for you to go over it with him at home.

After the homework discussion, the therapist inquired, "Is there anything important that you and I need to check-in on before Jeremy and I get started?" Ms. J. offered that she had seen Jeremy sitting alone on the tire swing with tears running down his cheeks. She said that she did not know what to say to him. So, she just gave him a big hug and told him that she loved him. The therapist recognized this as an opportunity to strengthen rapport after having had to give a tough message earlier about homework completion. The following specific praise was given to the mother: "You obviously have very good instincts. I think what he needed right then was physical comfort and reassurance that he was still loved."

Child's Work. This portion began with a review of playroom rules which included (a) modeling how disruptive behavior would be ignored and (b) reinforcing good listening skills. The therapist briefly reviewed the first section of the play therapy book and then read the remaining pages (prior to the termination section) in detail with Jeremy. The "Ups and Downs with Feelings Game" (Gesme, 1987; may be ordered by telephoning 1-612-938-9163) was used to teach Jeremy age-appropriate labels for feelings.

Child's Play. The therapist used child-directed play therapy process skills to build rapport and enhance self-esteem. At one point, Jeremy made a gun out of construction straws, and he began pretending to shoot the heads off of all the stuffed animals. Not wanting to reinforce escalating aggression, the therapist turned away from Jeremy and modeled nurturant behavior. The therapist gently stroked the bunny's ears while saying, "I like animals. I'm going to be nice to this rabbit. He likes it when I pet him softly." Recognizing that the therapist had turned away and was actively ignoring his aggressive behavior, Jeremy put down his sword and said, "I've got a good idea. I'll make some food for the rabbit with this clay." The therapist turned back to Jeremy and praised him for taking good care of the rabbit. Once Jeremy had been calm for a minute or so, the therapist offered the following delayed interpretation:

> I guess you were feeling angry when you were hurting the animals with your gun. This is a good place for you to talk about angry feelings using your words. When you show your anger by fighting or being rough with the toys, I have to turn around like this. But when you use your words to tell me that you feel angry, I won't have to turn away. Here are those cards we looked at earlier; show me which one is the way you felt when you were hurting the stuffed animals. What is that feeling called? Great job of talking about feelings!

Child's Play ended with Jeremy again helping to put away toys and receiving a good behavior prize.

Check-Out. Jeremy demonstrated to his mother his new skills for labeling feelings. She was given a homework assignment to read the play therapy book (except for the termination section) and to practice identifying feelings.

Session Three

Session Objectives: (a) Increase Jeremy's vocabulary for talking about feelings; (b) Begin discussion of family issues; and (c) Provide a safe and accepting environment to encourage self-disclosure.

Check-In. Immediately upon arrival, Ms. J. was asked about the homework assignment. She proudly told the therapist that she and Jeremy had read the play therapy book together twice and had been practicing "I feel..." statements during their car rides. The therapist praised Ms. J. for making the time to help her son. As the therapist stood up to move to the other room, Jeremy ran ahead and to the door and shouted, "I'll race ya!" The therapist held the door closed and said, "Remember, the rule is that we always walk to the playroom together." A "when-then" strategy was used to discourage Jeremy from running away: "When you take my hand, then I will open the door." The hand-holding was followed by labeled praise: "Thanks for listening and remembering our rule about walking together."

Child's Work. Child's Work began by reviewing last session's feeling cards and listening to an audiotape of songs about feelings. The "Talking, Feeling, and Doing Game" (Gardner, 1973; may be ordered by telephoning 1-800-648-8857) was played using cards preselected for family and loss themes. In response to a card that said, "Tell about a time when you felt scared," Jeremy said, "I was really scared when Leslie fell down." The therapist validated Jeremy's feeling with a reflective statement and offered him labeled praise, "That must have been very scary. Thank you for talking to me about your feelings. You get an extra chip for talking about a really hard thing." The therapist then asked in an animated voice, "Did you know that you can have more than one feeling at a time? When Leslie fell down, what else do you think that you might have felt besides scared? I have an idea. Let's take a look at our feelings cards." Jeremy picked a sad face with tears streaming down. To maintain his attention and cooperation, the therapist stamped Jeremy's hand and praised him for working hard. She then said, "Jeremy, please come over to the chalkboard with me. I need your help. Thanks for coming over. What do you think a person's face might look like if he felt sad and scared all at the same time?" The therapist proceeded to draw an outline of a face with a line down the middle and the features blank. Jeremy was invited to assist the therapist in drawing a sad feeling (e.g., tears) on the left side and an angry feeling (e.g., bared teeth) on the right side.

Child's Play. In Child's Play, Jeremy chose to continue playing the therapeutic game. The therapist used many descriptive and reflective statements as well as labeled praise. Jeremy seemed much more comfortable with the therapist this week and clearly enjoyed her attention. At the end of Child's Play, the therapist discussed with Jeremy the feedback she wanted to give to his mother. She told Jeremy that she would like to let his mother know that they had talked about feelings and about how you can have more than one at a time. The therapist was careful to tell Jeremy that what he had said about Leslie was private and would not be told to his mother. The therapist emphasized that he, of course, could tell his mother anything he wanted to about their therapy. Jeremy was asked if there was anything in particular that he did not want the therapist to talk about with his mother. He shook his head and shrugged his shoulders, indicating that it was fine to talk with his mother about the session.

Check-Out. Ms. J. was given feedback on the Child's Work accomplishments. She was asked to continue helping Jeremy with affective labels, particularly the concept of experiencing two feelings at once.

Session Four

Session Objectives: (a) Present age-appropriate information about death; (b) Recount specific details about Leslie's death; and (c) Provide opportunity for child to gain affective distance from sensitive material prior to end of session.

Check-In. The homework was reviewed with Ms. J. She again was praised for assisting Jeremy with his therapy. When asked if there was anything that the therapist needed to know about before beginning Jeremy's play therapy session, Ms. J. launched into a lengthy discussion of recent stressors. She said that she had been transferred to an office building across town. A long commute was required, and she had to leave the house early in the morning. She complained that Jeremy had been a "pill" in the mornings, refusing to get dressed and brush his teeth. In addition, she brought in a note from Jeremy's first grade teacher describing an explosive outburst in the cafeteria. As Ms. J. proceeded to vent frustration and discuss tangential details, Jeremy began to play disruptively with the toys, crashing cars and running them off of the table. Therapist attempts to get Ms. J. to balance her discussion with some positive feedback for Jeremy were only marginally successful. The therapist then became more directive and began to set limits on Ms. J.'s venting. This was accomplished by actively reflecting her concerns and by redirecting her to the issues at hand:

> (Therapist leans in closer and makes a time-out sign with her hands) Let me stop you right there for a minute. You just mentioned a number of important issues. It seems like things have been very stressful for you lately. And Jeremy's behavior certainly hasn't helped the situation. One factor that I want you to be aware of is that Jeremy is beginning to talk about some difficult issues in therapy. Re-experiencing the grief and guilt may lead to some temporary increases in his aggressive and disruptive behaviors. But, it could also be that Jeremy is simply showing the same sorts of behavior problems that he has had for a long time now. Unfortunately, we can't tackle all of the concerns that you

have with Jeremy at once. With only 12 weeks of therapy, we are going to have to stay focused on the goals that we outlined. I wish I had a quick and easy solution for you, but I don't. What I do know is that he is working hard and making some progress. It is important that I get to work with Jeremy right now so that we have enough time for his therapy. Perhaps we will have time to talk more about this later. I'm glad you told me about what is happening.

Child's Work. Recognizing that trauma resolution is facilitated by successive re-enactments or re-tellings of the traumatic event, the therapist decided to use materials in this session that would directly induce discussion about Leslie's death. The therapist chose to do this relatively early in treatment to ensure sufficient time for multiple re-enactments. By telling the story repeatedly or re-enacting it in play, the therapist expected that Jeremy would gain emotional distance from the event and that his distress would diminish.

To directly address Jeremy's grief issues, he was introduced to the children's grief workbook entitled, *When Someone Very Special Dies* (Heegaard, 1991; available by phoning 1-704-675-5909). Jeremy was very interested in this activity and asked frequent questions about the material. He and the therapist worked through the first several pages which present basic information about death (e.g., everything that lives eventually dies). Jeremy recalled that his pet hamster lived only one day. Discussing the hamster helped Jeremy assimilate the information about death being permanent and bodily functions ceasing. Further into the workbook, an opportunity was provided for Jeremy to tell about how someone very special in his life had died. He began telling about Leslie's death, and the therapist asked strategic questions that encouraged him to provide very specific details about the event (e.g., what each person was wearing, what the back yard looked like, what toys they had been playing with, who was home, what happened immediately before she fell down, what happened while she was lying down, what happened immediately afterwards).

Jeremy was given an opportunity to draw a picture in his workbook of how his sister died. When he said that he did not want to draw the picture, the therapist said, "I have a great idea. I'll send this book home with you and your mom. You can look at it together. If you feel like drawing a picture then, you can. I'm really proud of you for being brave and talking about what happened to Leslie. How are you feeling inside?" Jeremy answered by indicating that he was feeling tired. The therapist praised him for using his words to describe his feelings and agreed that this would be a good time to take a break. Before ending Child's Work, the therapist praised Jeremy for talking about Leslie's death and further reinforced this by giving him a "bravery certificate."

Child's Play. In this session, Child's Play served the important function of helping Jeremy to regain control of his emotions. After discussing the trauma of Leslie's death during Child's Work, Jeremy was feeling helpless, vulnerable, and fatigued. Child's Play allowed him to play with toys that were not affectively laden, thus distancing himself from negative feelings. Jeremy was able to lead the play and to have mastery experiences with constructional toys. The therapist provided continuous support for Jeremy's choice of activities and frequently praised him for his efforts and accomplishments. The Child's Play atmosphere was one in which Jeremy felt no pressure to discuss feelings or difficult issues. By the end of Child's Play, Jeremy was cheerful and energetic and seemed strong enough to transition from therapy to his daily routine. When asked, Jeremy gave permission to the therapist to talk with his mother about the grief workbook and to tell her that they had discussed Leslie's death.

Check-Out. Ms. J. was shown the work that was completed in Jeremy's grief workbook. She was asked to go over this work with him at home, not progressing past the point reached during Child's Work. Ms. J. was told that Jeremy had done a terrific job of talking about his sister's death in this session and that the therapist was pleased with his progress. Jeremy proudly displayed his bravery certificate to his mother.

Session Five

Session Objectives: (a) Continue to present age-appropriate information about death; (b) Recount specific details about Leslie's death and funeral; (c) Discuss and role-play appropriate ways to express anger; and (d) Provide opportunity for Jeremy to gain affective distance from sensitive material prior to end of session.

Check-In. When asked about Jeremy's homework assignment, Ms. J. indicated that she had not had time this week to look at his grief workbook with him. Upon further discussion, it became apparent that Ms. J. was avoiding the homework because she was worried that she might cry in front of Jeremy. The therapist reframed the crying as an appropriate modeling of the expression of grief. The mother seemed relieved and said that she would like to read the book with him this week. The therapist asked Ms. J. if she had noticed any changes in Jeremy's interest in playing with other children. Ms. J. reported that he seemed to be a little more sociable and had asked to have a neighbor boy spend the night. She added that defiant and aggressive behavior continued to be problematic.

Child's Work. The workbook *When Someone Very Special Dies* was completed. A section of the workbook was devoted to strategies for coping with feelings of anger (e.g., scribbling hard on a piece of paper and throwing it away, hitting a pillow). In addition, the Turtle Technique (see Chapter Four) was taught to Jeremy as a self-control tool he could use at home and at school when feeling angry. Jeremy received several handstamps and stickers for mastering elements of the turtle technique.

Child's Play. During Child's Play, Jeremy seemed fidgety and irritable. He complained often that there were not enough toys to play with and that he wished he was home so he could watch his favorite show on television. At one point, he headed toward the door and said, "I'm going to show this picture to my mom." The therapist sat with her back to the door and replied, "The rule is that we have to stay in the playroom until our playtime is over. If you want, I'll put the picture right here by the door so we'll remember to take it to your mom then." Jeremy responded by stomping his feet, crossing his arms, and extending his lower lip. He went to the other side of the playroom and looked away from the therapist.

The therapist remained with her back to the door and ignored Jeremy's disruptive behavior. She began describing her own coloring activity with enthusiasm. When Jeremy did not orient in her direction after a minute or so, she switched activities and began to build an airplane with the toys. As she increased her animation and began to fly her airplane, Jeremy said, "I want an airplane." The therapist returned her attention to Jeremy and said, "Thanks for coming back to play with me. I would be happy to share my airplane with you."

After several minutes of leading the play, Jeremy spontaneously stood up and began to run back and forth with the airplane. He jumped onto a chair so he could make his plane fly high and then screeched as he jumped down. Because Jeremy's behavior was becoming too active and out of control, the therapist displayed her handstamp and prompted him to "do the turtle." Wanting the reward, Jeremy complied quickly and the therapist praised him for being able to calm himself down. While Jeremy was relaxing "inside his shell," the therapist reminded him of the playroom rule that no one can get hurt. She explained that she was worried that he might hurt himself when he was running and jumping indoors. The therapist went on to tell Jeremy that she cared very much about him and wanted him to stay safe.

In response to the therapist's safety message, Jeremy replied, "I don't know why you care about me. Everybody else thinks I killed my sister." The therapist asked, "Do you think you killed your sister?" Jeremy answered, "Maybe." Upon further questioning, Jeremy revealed that he felt he should have called 911 but that he was too scared. Then, the therapist leaned closer to Jeremy and said, "I want you to listen very closely to what I'm about to tell you. This is important. You did not kill your sister. Leslie's death is NOT YOUR FAULT. It was an accident. Even if you had called 911, Leslie would have died. It was an accident. It was not your fault." The therapist went on to ask Jeremy if he understood what she had just said. She gave him an opportunity to talk more about those thoughts and feelings but he declined. Jeremy was praised for being brave and talking about Leslie's death. Child's Play ended with several minutes of child-directed play. The therapist also indicated to Jeremy that she would like to talk with his mother on the phone this week about the progress he was making in talking about Leslie. She asked him whether there was anything that he did not want the therapist to mention to his mother, and he responded negatively.

Check-Out. Jeremy was given the opportunity to practice doing the turtle for his mother during the Check-Out time. Ms. J. was given two handouts on the Turtle Technique: one for her own use at home and one to be given to Jeremy's classroom teacher. For her first homework assignment, Ms. J. was asked to prompt and reinforce Jeremy for using the Turtle Technique throughout the week. She was told that he should "overpractice" doing the turtle, rehearsing it both when he is calm and receptive and when he is displaying disruptive behavior. As a second homework assignment, Ms. J. was asked to meet with Jeremy's teacher to review the turtle technique handout, explaining that Jeremy could use this technique to regain self-control at school. Ms. J. was asked to encourage the teacher to employ this strategy with all of the students in the class so that Jeremy would not feel self-conscious and singled out. Ms. J.'s third homework assignment was to read with Jeremy the book, *When Someone Very Special Dies.*

Telephone Call. Shortly after the session was over, the therapist telephoned Ms. J. to discuss Jeremy's guilt feelings. The therapist chose to address this in a telephone call rather than during the session because she did not feel that it was appropriate for Jeremy to be present during this discussion. Ms. J. was told that Jeremy appears to blame himself for his sister's death. She was asked whether she felt that Jeremy was responsible for Leslie's death. She responded, "Of course not! If anyone is to blame, it's me. I shouldn't have expected him to watch her." The therapist explained that in order for Jeremy to cope with his sister's death, he needed to let go of any feelings of responsibility. The therapist asked Ms. J. if she would be willing to tell Jeremy that the death was not his fault. She said that she had already done that but would be willing to do it again. The therapist explained that Jeremy needed to hear that message many times in order to internalize it. She told Ms. J. that she would have an opportunity to give Jeremy this message again in the next play therapy session.

Session Six

Session Objectives: (a) Teach Jeremy the concept of "guilt;" (b) Emphasize that Leslie's death was not his fault; and (c) Bolster Jeremy's self-esteem.

Check-In. Ms. J.'s three homework assignments were reviewed, and she was praised for her follow-through. She offered that when reading the grief workbook she asked Jeremy if he felt responsible for Leslie's death. He reportedly told her that he wished he had called 911. Ms. J. proudly recounted to the therapist how she responded by telling him that Leslie's death was not his fault, and that she is the one who should have called 911 more quickly. The therapist praised Jeremy for talking about feelings and praised Ms. J. for giving Jeremy the message he needed to hear.

Child's Work. To assist Jeremy in further processing his feelings of responsibility, the therapist used an exercise to teach him the affective label of "guilt." Prior to this exercise, the only descriptive labels he had for those feelings were "bad" and "sad." To help him differentiate his emotions, a series of age-appropriate examples of situations in which a child might feel guilty was generated (e.g., when a child breaks his mother's favorite dish, when a child strikes out at bat and his team loses). Jeremy then was asked to join the therapist at the chalkboard. The therapist asked Jeremy to draw a line down the middle of the board. On one side, they generated a list of things that a seven-year-old boy is able to do (e.g., ride his bicycle, make his bed). On the other side, they generated a list of things that a seven-year-old boy is unable to do (e.g., drive a car, repair the roof). The critical item on this list was that young boys could not always stop accidents from happening. This was another method of emphasizing that Leslie's death was not Jeremy's fault. In order for Jeremy to accept that he was not to blame, he needed to view himself less negatively. To bolster his self-esteem, the book, *I Like Me!*, was read and discussed with Jeremy. He was asked to generate three good things about himself.

Child's Play. During the child-directed activity, the therapist provided numerous statements of labeled praise for Jeremy's efforts, accomplishments, and attributes. Occasionally, Jeremy rejected the therapist's praises by arguing that they were not true. The therapist recognized that due to his low self-esteem, accepting compliments would be a gradual process for Jeremy. Although he rejected these statements of praise in this session, the therapist believed that they still would have a cumulative impact on his self-esteem. Thus, she chose not to reinforce his protests by debating the accuracy of the praise, and she continued to offer genuine praise.

Check-Out. Ms. J. was asked to read *I Like Me!* with Jeremy at home and to do the following self-esteem exercise each night: "Ask Jeremy to think of three things he did well that day. Then tell Jeremy three things that you like about him."

Session Seven

Session Objectives: (a) Review the concept of "guilt;" (b) Continue emphasizing that Leslie's death was not his fault; (c) Bolster Jeremy's self-esteem; and (d) Introduce termination issues.

Check-In. The previous session's homework assignment was reviewed with Ms. J. She indicated that she had been able to do the self-esteem exercise only three times the previous week because of her hectic work schedule. The therapist emphasized that with only five sessions remaining, daily homework is particularly important.

Child's Work. To review the concept of guilt, the technique of "special game rules" was employed. Jeremy was told that he and the therapist would play a special game of "trash can basketball." The rules of this special game were that each player would have to talk about something that could make a person feel guilty before getting a turn to throw.

After the game, the therapist used a cognitive-behavioral strategy to help Jeremy reduce the maladaptive cognition that he was responsible for his sister's death. On one sheet of paper, the therapist wrote the dysfunctional thought, "My sister died because I didn't call 911." The following coping statement was written on a second sheet of paper: "Leslie's death was NOT my fault." To help Jeremy understand the importance of diminishing the maladaptive thought while enhancing the coping statement, the therapist used a copy machine. Jeremy was invited to assist the therapist in using the enlargement function to blow up the coping statement, then using the reduction function to shrink the maladaptive thought. After returning to the play-room, Jeremy was encouraged to tear up the tiny maladaptive thought and throw it in the trash can. The enlarged coping statement was given to Jeremy so that he could post it promi-nently in his bedroom.

To assist Jeremy in understanding and cooperating with upcoming changes in play therapy, Jeremy was informed that his mother was going to start being included in Child's Work. He was told that the therapist was going to teach his mother a really fun way to play with him that would help them get along better at home. It was explained to him that for the next few ses-sions the therapist would watch how he and his mother played together and would give her suggestions for alternative ways to play. He was reassured that he would still get to have his individual play time with the therapist. The process of ending therapy was introduced to Jeremy by reading the termination section of *A Child's First Book About Play Therapy*. Furthermore, Jeremy and the therapist drew a picture of a staircase with each stair represent-ing one of the five remaining treatment sessions (see Appendix). At the top of the stairs was a picture depicting the end-of-treatment party. In each remaining session, Jeremy would be given an opportunity to draw himself and the therapist on the step corresponding to that treat-ment session. This strategy was designed to help Jeremy visualize the number of sessions remaining.

Child's Play. After the work addressing loss and termination issues, Jeremy continued to work through these themes in his child-directed play. He selected puppets and asked the ther-apist to play the role of the father while he played the role of the son. Jeremy enacted a series of scenes in which, for various reasons, he was parted from his father. The therapist noticed that all of the scenes involved an abrupt separation. The following interpretation was offered: "Your puppet hasn't had a chance to say goodbye to my puppet. It's hard when you don't get to say goodbye. I wonder if anybody has ever left you without saying goodbye." Jeremy talked about a time in which his mother went to work while he was asleep, and when he woke up a babysitter was there. The therapist used strategic interpretations to help Jeremy realize that he did not have an opportunity to say goodbye to his sister and father. Jeremy used the puppets to act out parting scenes with both Leslie and his father, thus beginning to gain some closure on those relationships.

Check-Out. Ms. J. was instructed to attend Session Eight without Jeremy so that she could be taught a set of "play therapy" skills. Her homework assignment for this week was to read along with Jeremy the termination section of the play therapy book.

Session Eight

Session Objectives: (a) Discuss with Ms. J. the child-directed interaction play therapy skills; (b) Role-play the skills with Ms. J.; and (c) Begin assigning home practice of special playtime skills.

Check-In. Session Eight was the only session that did not conform to the structure out-lined in Chapter Two. Ms. J. attended this session alone so that the therapist could have her undivided attention while presenting and role-playing the basic skills for child-directed play. Immediately upon arrival, Ms. J. was asked about her completion of the previous week's homework assignment. She indicated that she and Jeremy had looked at the play therapy book together twice and that he seemed very interested in the "long goodbye." The therapist praised Ms. J. for completing the homework and asked if there was anything important that should be discussed before beginning to talk about child-directed play. Ms. J. remarked that she felt that Jeremy was more successful in controlling his anger this week and had usually been responsive to her prompts to "do the turtle." The therapist presented the rules and rationales for each of the child-directed play therapy process skills (see Chapter Seven). Ms. J. was then invited to role-play the skills with the therapist. She appeared to be enthusiastic about beginning her practice sessions at home.

Check-Out. Ms. J. was given a handout on child-directed play skills (see Appendix) and was given the homework assignment to begin practicing these skills in a daily 5- to 10-minute special playtime with Jeremy using construction toys. She was also given a Special Playtime Homework Sheet for recording purposes (see Appendix).

Session Nine

Session Objectives: (a) Coach Ms. J. in child-directed play skills; and (b) Begin decreasing time spent in Child's Play in anticipation of termination.

Check-In. Ms. J. indicated that she had been able to do special playtime with Jeremy on five evenings during the week and that he appeared to look forward to their time together. The therapist briefly problem-solved with her regarding issues that came up during the play and about her selection of activities. Ms. J. indicated that on one evening, she and Jeremy had tossed the football to each other for their special playtime. The therapist acknowledged that this sounded as though it had been enjoyable and good quality time, but emphasized that this type of activity is not well-suited to play therapy. Possible alternative activities were discussed. The change in session structure was presented to Jeremy and his mother. Jeremy was told that he and his mother would have special playtime while the therapist coached Ms. J. Jeremy was instructed to pretend that he could not hear or see the therapist during coaching and was reminded that he would have an opportunity later to spend time with the therapist alone.

Coding. Ms. J.'s special playtime skills were recorded during a five-minute coding session. Prior to the coding, Ms. J. was prompted to review with Jeremy the special playtime rules (e.g., he must stay in the playroom; she will turn and ignore if he is disruptive). Although she made no critical remarks and gave no directions during the coding period, she was noted to ask numerous questions. Her overall rate of speech was low, with long silences between her descriptive comments. She tended to observe passively rather than involve herself in her son's play. Ms. J. praised Jeremy twice during the five-minute recording period. Based on this information, the therapist decided to focus attention during coaching on increasing comfort with descriptions and promoting imitation.

Coaching. The majority of the session was devoted to direct coaching of special playtime skills. Ms. J. appeared nervous at first and hesitant to speak for fear of making a mistake. With frequent encouragement from the therapist, she greatly increased her overall rate of speech. By the end of the coaching period, she displayed good use of description and imitation, but continued to have problems with questions. Despite being instructed to pretend that the therapist was invisible during coaching, Jeremy attempted to obtain therapist attention by asking questions (e.g., "Can you get out the fire truck that we played with last time?"). The therapist ignored these overtures and Jeremy quickly re-engaged in the play with his mother.

Child's Work/Child's Play. Jeremy's individual time with the therapist was reduced to a 15-minute session. The therapist encouraged Jeremy to talk about his feelings concerning his special playtime sessions at home. He told the therapist that he really enjoyed special playtime but that his mother selected "stupid" toys to play with (i.e., no video games, no guns). The therapist reviewed the goals of special playtime and explained that only certain toys are allowed. She asked Jeremy to generate ideas for appropriate toys that stimulated his interest. Jeremy and the therapist also discussed how "funny" it seemed to have the therapist watching him and his mother play together and how he felt when the therapist did not respond to his questions during coaching. The balance of the time was spent in reviewing the "staircase to termination" and engaging in child-directed play.

Check-Out. Results of the coding were shared with Ms. J. She was encouraged to concentrate hard on catching herself asking questions and to restate each question as a description or reflection each time she caught it. Ms. J. was given the homework assignment to continue practicing her child-directed play skills in a daily 5- to 10-minute special playtime with Jeremy using construction toys. A homework sheet was again provided for recording daily practice.

Session Ten

Session Objectives: (a) Continue coaching Ms. J. in child-directed play skills; and (b) Further decrease time spent in Child's Play in anticipation of termination.

Check-In. When the therapist inquired about Ms. J.'s homework completion, she reported that she had not had many opportunities to practice because Jeremy had really been a "handful" this week. She launched into an animated account of all of the ways Jeremy had made her life difficult. Recognizing that Jeremy was feeling overwhelmed by his mother's criticism in the session, the therapist redirected Ms. J. to balance her feedback with acknowledgements of his successes. Further discussion revealed that Ms. J. had withheld special playtime on several days as punishment for misbehavior. The therapist empathized with the fact that it is difficult to set aside angry feelings to have playtime. However, Ms. J. was urged to think of special playtime as therapy that is particularly needed when Jeremy is having a difficult day. She was told that special playtime is not a privilege to be withheld.

Coding. During the five-minute coding period, Ms. J. was observed to use many more descriptive statements than she had the previous week. Although she continued to ask questions, particularly when attempting to reflect, she appeared to recognize them and was able to restate a few. Unfortunately, her rate of praise remained low. The few instances of praise that she provided were unlabeled. Based on this information, the therapist decided to focus the coaching on reflective statements and labeled praise.

Coaching. To assist Ms. J. in increasing her rate of reflections, the therapist conducted a special exercise in which Ms. J. was asked to reflect every appropriate verbalization made by Jeremy during a three-minute period. Her first few reflections sounded like questions because of the voice inflection at the end. The therapist pointed this out to her by saying, "Do you hear that question mark in your voice? Say it like it is a fact." As Ms. J. became more proficient at reflecting, Jeremy spoke to her more. The therapist observed, "Your reflections are working. He's talking to you more today than he did last week." Each time Ms. J. used an unlabeled praise, the therapist provided a prompt such as, "Thanks for what?," "What's nice about that?," and "Good job of what?" By the end of the coaching session, Ms. J. recognized how she could use labeled praise to encourage Jeremy to sit still, play gently with the toys, and share.

At one point during the session, Jeremy became bossy, demanding that his mother construct a tower while he watched. The coaching proceeded as follows:

Jeremy: [bossy, loud tone] *"Make it higher. Hurry up!"*

Therapist: [quickly] *"Ignore that. Turn around. Just because he is supposed to lead the play does not mean you have to do everything he says. If you make it higher right now, you will reward his bossiness. Just describe your own play. That's it."*

Jeremy: [bossy and louder] *"I said make it higher!"*

Therapist: *"Good ignoring. As soon as he's quiet, turn back around and say, 'If you ask me nicely, I will build it higher.'"*

Ms. J.: [turns and repeats therapist's words]

Jeremy: [using a quiet voice] *"Make it higher, please."*

Therapist: *He did it so give him a labeled praise. Say, "Thanks for using good manners. I like to do things for you when you ask me nicely."*

Ms. J.: [repeats praise]

Therapist: *"Great job of teaching him to use better manners."*

Through the coaching, Ms. J. recognized how she could use her attention strategically to promote prosocial behavior in her son.

Child's Work/Child's Play. Jeremy's individual time with the therapist was reduced to a 10-minute session. After the Staircase to Termination picture was reviewed, the therapist allowed Jeremy to lead the play. At one point, Jeremy used polite manners to ask the therapist to hand him a marker. The therapist responded by saying, "I'm glad to hear you say 'please.' Would you mind if I tell your mother about your good manners when we meet with her in a few minutes?"

Check-Out. Results of the coding were reviewed with Ms. J. She was excited to see that she had made good progress in describing and imitating. Again, Ms. J. was given the homework assignment to continue practicing her child-directed play skills in a daily 5- to 10-minute special playtime with Jeremy. She was encouraged to look hard for praiseworthy behavior and to practice labeling her praise. She was again encouraged to make herself stop and restate her questions. Ms. J. was reminded that the next session would be expanded to one and a half hours to allow for post-treatment evaluation procedures.

Session Eleven

Session Objectives: (a) Coach Ms. J. in child-directed play skills; (b) Further decrease time spent in Child's Play in anticipation of termination; (c) Have family complete post-treatment measures; and (d) Plan next session's termination ritual with Jeremy.

Check-In. During Check-In, Ms. J. proudly reported that she had not missed a single day of her special playtime homework. After praising her, the therapist asked Ms. J. if she had noticed herself using the skills outside of special playtime. She remarked that the skills were becoming a "habit." She indicated that when they had visited her father, he had commented that she seemed like she was enjoying Jeremy a lot more these days. To instill the expectation of improvements, Ms. J. was asked to describe any positive changes in Jeremy's behavior that had resulted from her daily special playtime. She reported that he seemed to enjoy spending time with her more than he had in the past. Prior to the end of Check-in, Jeremy was praised for playing quietly and not interrupting.

Post-treatment Evaluation. Ms. J. was asked to complete the same measures she completed before treatment: the Child Behavior Checklist and Eyberg Child Behavior Inventory. While she completed these measures, the therapist administered the Children's Depression

Inventory and the Harter self-esteem measure to Jeremy. Ms. J. was given a copy of the CBCL to give to Jeremy's teacher.

Coding. During the five-minute coding period, Ms. J. demonstrated remarkable improvement in praising. Whereas the week before she had praised Jeremy only four times (all unlabeled) during their five-minute coded interaction, this week she gave him seven labeled and five unlabeled statements of praise. Her questions were reduced to three, and she demonstrated good use of reflections, imitation, and descriptions.

Coaching. To support Ms. J.'s sense of parenting competency, coaching in this session emphasized her mastery. The therapist looked for opportunities to offer observations on the positive impact that her skills were having on Jeremy. At one point during the session, Jeremy said, "Look at this neat car I built!" After Ms. J. affirmed Jeremy's positive self-statement, the therapist commented that statements like that were indicative of improved self-esteem. The self-esteem improvement was credited to Ms. J. and attributed to her consistent home practice.

Child's Work/Child's Play. The first 10 minutes of Child's Play were spent reviewing the Staircase to Termination and planning the termination party. Jeremy was enthused at the prospect of eating cake and ice cream. The last five minutes were spent in child-directed play.

Check-Out. During Check-Out, Ms. J. indicated that she felt that Jeremy would benefit from additional sessions and inquired about whether the next session would have to be his last. The idea of booster sessions was mentioned to Ms. J., and she was reminded that the therapist would be reviewing Jeremy's progress with her next week to discuss any additional treatment needs. Ms. J. was given the homework assignment to continue practicing her child-directed play skills in a daily 5- to 10-minute special playtime with Jeremy. She was reminded to have the teacher fill out the CBCL form and give it to Ms. J. so that she could bring it to the next session.

Session Twelve

Session Objectives: (a) Complete termination rituals with both Ms. J. and Jeremy; and (b) Make any needed referrals for additional services.

Check-In. In this session 20 minutes were devoted to Check-In. Ms. J. was given a copy of Jeremy's treatment plan (see Table 10-2), and the therapist went over it with her in detail, emphasizing the work accomplished. Pre- to post-treatment changes on measures were also reviewed. Progress made toward treatment goals was highlighted, and a realistic assessment was offered of Jeremy's continuing needs. He displayed clinically significant improvements on measures of depression, self-esteem, and withdrawal. Much smaller magnitude improvements were found on measures of disruptive behavior (e.g., noncompliance with parental commands) and social problems (e.g., aggression toward peers). A summary of pre- to post-treatment changes on measures is presented in Table 10-3. In reviewing the post-treatment data, Ms. J. was advised that Jeremy made substantial progress in dealing with the immediate crisis of his sister's death. It was explained to Ms. J. that Jeremy was then ready to benefit from a social skills group and a behavior management program to address remaining concerns. She was given appropriate referrals for both of these services.

To enhance Ms. J.'s sense of competence and encourage her to continue using her new skills, the therapist praised her for the following: (a) attending sessions regularly, (b) completing homework assignments, (c) giving Jeremy a clearer message that he was not to blame for Leslie's death, and (d) developing excellent child-directed play skills.

Child's Work. A 10-minute period was devoted to reviewing the course of treatment with Jeremy. Together, Jeremy and the therapist looked at the materials that the therapist had placed around the room, remembering the issues and skills associated with each (e.g., experiencing two feelings at once, practicing the Turtle Technique, understanding guilt). Materials included *A Child's First Book About Play Therapy,* "The Talking, Feeling, and Doing Game," the grief workbook, puppets, feeling cards and audiotape, chalkboard with a face displaying two emotions, and the *I Like Me!* book. Jeremy was praised for all of the hard work he accomplished in therapy.

Child's Play. Approximately 20 minutes were devoted to the termination party. The therapist and Jeremy shared a small cake and made goodbye cards to exchange with each other. At one point during the party, Jeremy became overly-excited, running around the room and smearing cake on his face. The therapist responded by prompting Jeremy to do the turtle. At first, he did not respond. Then, the therapist said, "When you do the turtle, then I will give you a special prize." Jeremy calmed and the therapist reminded him that the playroom rules are still in effect, even during the party. Upon receiving his prize, Jeremy engaged in more appropriate behavior. Jeremy received a blue ribbon for his accomplishments in therapy and was invited to take some cake to his mother.

Check-Out. During the final 10 minutes of the session, Ms. J. was reminded that it is important for her to continue practicing her child-directed play skills on a daily basis. She was told that she could help Jeremy to maintain his gains and improve further by continuing to do special playtime on a daily basis for many years to come. When goodbyes were being said, Jeremy appeared tearful and said that he would like to visit again next week. The therapist responded by saying, "I'll miss you too. Perhaps you would like to call me on the telephone to tell me how you're doing. Would that be alright with you, Ms. J.?" The therapist shook hands with Ms. J. and Jeremy. Ms. J. was reminded that she was welcome to call and schedule follow-up appointments as needed.

Table 10-3. Summary of Pre- to Post-treatment Changes on Measures

Scale	Pre-Tx	Post-Tx
Child Behavior Checklist (parent report)		
Internalizing	T = 77	T = 67
Externalizing	T = 73	T = 71
Withdrawn	T = 84	T = 65
Somatic Complaints	T = 56	T = 56
Anxious/Depressed	T = 81	T = 66
Social Problems	T = 70	T = 67
Thought Problems	T = 67	T = 65
Attention Problems	T = 65	T = 60
Delinquent Behavior	T = 63	T = 59
Aggressive Behavior	T = 80	T = 75
Sex Problems	T = 50	T = 50
Eyberg Child Behavior Inventory		
Problem Score	20	15
Intensity Score	153	135
Children's Depression Inventory		
Total CDI Raw Score	T = 67	T = 57
Negative Mood	T = 70	T = 60
Interpersonal Problems	T = 57	T = 59
Ineffectiveness	T = 54	T = 55
Anhedonia	T = 67	T = 58
Negative Self-Esteem	T = 62	T = 55
Harter		
Cognitive Competence	3.67	3.67
Peer Acceptance	2.00	2.50
Physical Competence	3.83	3.67
Maternal Acceptance	1.33	3.00
Child Behavior Checklist (teacher report)		
Internalizing	T = 75	T = 68
Externalizing	T = 61	T = 63
Withdrawn	T = 83	T = 65
Somatic Complaints	T = 50	T = 50
Anxious/Depressed	T = 71	T = 66
Social Problems	T = 76	T = 68
Thought Problems	T = 58	T = 60
Attention Problems	T = 61	T = 64
Delinquent Behavior	T = 50	T = 50
Aggressive Behavior	T = 63	T = 61

APPENDIX

Play Therapy Star Chart

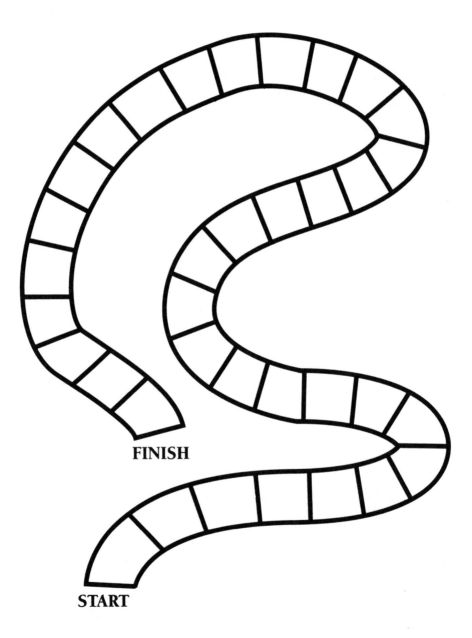

FINISH

START

Eyberg Child Behavior Inventory

Rater's Name: _____   Child's Name: _____

Relationship to Child: _____   Child's Age: _____

Date of Rating: _____   Birthdate: _____

Directions: Below is a series of phrases that describe children's behavior. Please (1) circle the number describing how often the behavior currently occurs with your child, and (2) circle either "yes" or "no" to indicate whether the behavior is currently a problem.

		How often does this occur with your child?							*Is this a problem for you?*	
		Never	**Seldom**	**Sometimes**	**Often**	**Always**				
1.	Dawdles in getting dressed	1	2	3	4	5	6	7	Yes	No
2.	Dawdles or lingers at mealtime	1	2	3	4	5	6	7	Yes	No
3.	Has poor table manners	1	2	3	4	5	6	7	Yes	No
4.	Refuses to eat food presented	1	2	3	4	5	6	7	Yes	No
5.	Refuses to do chores when asked	1	2	3	4	5	6	7	Yes	No
6.	Slow in getting ready for bed	1	2	3	4	5	6	7	Yes	No
7.	Refuses to go to bed on time	1	2	3	4	5	6	7	Yes	No
8.	Does not obey house rules on his own	1	2	3	4	5	6	7	Yes	No
9.	Refuses to obey until threatened with punishment	1	2	3	4	5	6	7	Yes	No
10.	Acts defiant when told to do something	1	2	3	4	5	6	7	Yes	No
11.	Argues with parents about rules	1	2	3	4	5	6	7	Yes	No
12.	Gets angry when doesn't get his own way	1	2	3	4	5	6	7	Yes	No
13.	Has temper tantrums	1	2	3	4	5	6	7	Yes	No
14.	Sasses adults	1	2	3	4	5	6	7	Yes	No
15.	Whines	1	2	3	4	5	6	7	Yes	No
16.	Cries easily	1	2	3	4	5	6	7	Yes	No
17.	Yells or screams	1	2	3	4	5	6	7	Yes	No
18.	Hits parents	1	2	3	4	5	6	7	Yes	No
19.	Destroys toys and other objects	1	2	3	4	5	6	7	Yes	No
20.	Is careless with toys and other objects	1	2	3	4	5	6	7	Yes	No
21.	Steals	1	2	3	4	5	6	7	Yes	No
22.	Lies	1	2	3	4	5	6	7	Yes	No
23.	Teases or provokes other children	1	2	3	4	5	6	7	Yes	No
24.	Verbally fights with friends his own age	1	2	3	4	5	6	7	Yes	No
25.	Verbally fights with siblings	1	2	3	4	5	6	7	Yes	No
26.	Physically fights with friends	1	2	3	4	5	6	7	Yes	No
27.	Physically fights with siblings	1	2	3	4	5	6	7	Yes	No
28.	Constantly seeks attention	1	2	3	4	5	6	7	Yes	No
29.	Interrupts	1	2	3	4	5	6	7	Yes	No
30.	Is easily distracted	1	2	3	4	5	6	7	Yes	No
31.	Has short attention span	1	2	3	4	5	6	7	Yes	No
32.	Fails to finish tasks or projects	1	2	3	4	5	6	7	Yes	No
33.	Has difficulty entertaining himself	1	2	3	4	5	6	7	Yes	No
34.	Has difficulty concentrating	1	2	3	4	5	6	7	Yes	No
35.	Is overactive or restless	1	2	3	4	5	6	7	Yes	No
36.	Wets the bed	1	2	3	4	5	6	7	Yes	No

Sutter-Eyberg Student Behavior Inventory

Rater's Name: _____ Child's Name: _____

Relationship to Child: _____ Child's Age: _____

Date of Rating: _____ Birthdate: _____

Directions: Below is a series of phrases that describe children's behavior. Please (1) circle the number describing how often the behavior currently occurs with your child, and (2) circle either "yes" or "no" to indicate whether the behavior is currently a problem.

		How often does this occur with your child?		*Is this a problem for you?*	
		Never Seldom Sometimes Often Always			
1.	Dawdles in obeying rules	1 2 3 4 5 6 7		Yes	No
2.	Argues with teachers about rules	1 2 3 4 5 6 7		Yes	No
3.	Has difficulty accepting criticism	1 2 3 4 5 6 7		Yes	No
4.	Does not obey school rules	1 2 3 4 5 6 7		Yes	No
5.	Refuses to obey until threatened with punishment	1 2 3 4 5 6 7		Yes	No
6.	Gets angry when doesn't get own way	1 2 3 4 5 6 7		Yes	No
7.	Acts defiant when told to do something	1 2 3 4 5 6 7		Yes	No
8.	Has temper tantrums	1 2 3 4 5 6 7		Yes	No
9.	Sasses teacher(s)	1 2 3 4 5 6 7		Yes	No
10.	Whines	1 2 3 4 5 6 7		Yes	No
11.	Cries	1 2 3 4 5 6 7		Yes	No
12.	Pouts	1 2 3 4 5 6 7		Yes	No
13.	Yells or screams	1 2 3 4 5 6 7		Yes	No
14.	Hits teacher(s)	1 2 3 4 5 6 7		Yes	No
15.	Is careless with books and other objects	1 2 3 4 5 6 7		Yes	No
16.	Destroys books and other objects	1 2 3 4 5 6 7		Yes	No
17.	Steals	1 2 3 4 5 6 7		Yes	No
18.	Lies	1 2 3 4 5 6 7		Yes	No
19.	Makes noises in class	1 2 3 4 5 6 7		Yes	No
20.	Teases or provokes other students	1 2 3 4 5 6 7		Yes	No
21.	Acts bossy with other students	1 2 3 4 5 6 7		Yes	No
22.	Verbally fights with other students	1 2 3 4 5 6 7		Yes	No
23.	Physically fights with other students	1 2 3 4 5 6 7		Yes	No
24.	Demands teacher attention	1 2 3 4 5 6 7		Yes	No
25.	Interrupts teachers	1 2 3 4 5 6 7		Yes	No
26.	Interrupts other students	1 2 3 4 5 6 7		Yes	No
27.	Has difficulty entering groups	1 2 3 4 5 6 7		Yes	No
28.	Has difficulty sharing materials	1 2 3 4 5 6 7		Yes	No
29.	Is uncooperative in group activities	1 2 3 4 5 6 7		Yes	No
30.	Blames others for problem behaviors	1 2 3 4 5 6 7		Yes	No
31.	Is easily distracted	1 2 3 4 5 6 7		Yes	No
32.	Has difficulty staying on task	1 2 3 4 5 6 7		Yes	No
33.	Acts frustrated with difficult tasks	1 2 3 4 5 6 7		Yes	No
34.	Fails to finish tasks or projects	1 2 3 4 5 6 7		Yes	No
35.	Impulsive, acts before thinking	1 2 3 4 5 6 7		Yes	No
36.	Is over-active or restless	1 2 3 4 5 6 7		Yes	No

Client Awareness Form

I have applied for services for my child, _____, at _____ (clinic name), with _____ (practitioner's name), a Licensed Psychologist. I understand and agree to the following:

1. No information or reports will be released without my specific written consent, except in the following cases:

    a. In an emergency, I authorize _____ (practitioner's name) to obtain or release information as needed to handle the emergency.

    b. I am aware that the law requires that _____ (practitioner's name) report any incidents of suspected child abuse or intention to injure myself or other people.

    c. I am aware that noncustodial parents may have the right to view their children's treatment records.

    d. I am aware that, in some circumstances, _____ (practitioner's name) records may be subpoenaed by the Court.

2. A $_____ evaluation fee and a $_____ per session fee for treatment services will be charged:

    a. I will pay these fees at the time services are rendered, unless arrangements are made otherwise.

    b. If I have insurance and want to file such claims for reimbursement, I understand that _____ (practitioner's name) is required to indicate dates of service, charge, and diagnosis on the insurance claim.

    c. I understand that I am fully responsible for payment of any fees that my insurance company declines to reimburse.

    d. I understand that any unpaid delinquent fees may be turned over to a collection agent.

    e. I will give 24-hour notice to cancel an appointment which has been made for me. This policy is necessary to ensure that families may be seen in a timely fashion and appointment times are not wasted on late cancellations and "no shows."

3. I understand that _____ adheres to the American Psychological Association Code of Ethics for Psychologists.

4. I understand that if I am dissatisfied with services received from _____, I can contact the State Board of License Examiners to make an inquiry or lodge a complaint.

5. I understand that _____ does not provide 24-hour per day on-call emergency services. In case of an emergency, I may request that the answering service attempt to locate _____, but I understand that she may not be immediately available. In a crisis, I may request assistance from _____

Mother's Signature: _____ Date: _____

Father's Signature: _____ Date: _____

Child's Signature: _____ Date: _____

Witness' Signature: _____ Date: _____

Attendance Contract

I agree to bring my child to play therapy sessions for the next 11 weeks. If I cannot attend because of illness or a scheduling conflict, I agree to call and reschedule the session as soon as possible, preferably within the same week. I understand that the success of this therapy is dependent upon my child's regular attendance.

Signed: _____   Date: _____

Treatment Plan Worksheet
(Where blank, therapist and/or parent may fill in)

Child's Name: _____   Date: _____

Goal #1: _____

Goal #2: _____

Goal #3: _____

Session #	Child's Work Activity	Homework Assignment
1	*A Child's First Book About Play Therapy* book Practice listening skills Review playroom rules	Read play therapy book
2	Complete *A Child's First Book About Play Therapy* book Review listening skills and playroom rules Exercise for labeling feelings	Continue reading play therapy book Practice labeling feelings
3		
4		
5		
6		

(continued)

Treatment Plan Worksheet (Continued)

Session #	Child's Work Activity	Homework Assignment
7	Read termination section of play therapy book	Read termination section of play therapy book
8	Teach parents play therapy skills (No child present)	Practice "special playtime" for 5 minutes each day
9	Coach parents in play therapy skills as they interact with child	Practice "special playtime" for 5 minutes each day
10	Coach parents in play therapy skills as they interact with child	Practice "special playtime" for 5 minutes each day
11	Coach parents in play therapy skills as they interact with child	Practice "special playtime" for 5 minutes each day
12	Review child's progress toward goals Termination rituals (e.g., party)	

"Do" and "Don't" Skills for Special Playtime
Parent Handout

Rule	Reason	Examples
Do *Describe* appropriate behavior.	Allows child to lead Shows child you're interested Teaches concepts Models speech Holds child's attention Organizes child's thoughts about play	That's a red block. You're making a tower. You drew a smiling face. The cowboy looks happy.
Do *Reflect* appropriate talk.	Doesn't control the conversation Shows child you're really listening Demonstrates acceptance and understanding Improves child's speech Increases verbal communication	**Child:** *I made a star.* **Parent:** *Yes, you made a star.* **Child:** *The camel got bumps on top.* **Parent:** *It has two humps on its back.* **Child:** *I like to play with this castle.* **Parent:** *This is a fun castle to play with.*
Do *Imitate* appropriate play.	Lets child lead Approves child's choice of play Shows child you are involved Shows child how to play with others (forms basis of taking turns) Tends to increase child's imitation of what you do	**Child:** *I'm putting baby to bed.* **Parent:** *I'll put sister to bed too.* **Child:** *I'm making a sun in the sky.* **Parent:** *I'm going to put a sun in my picture too.*
Do *Praise* appropriate behavior.	Causes the behavior to increase Lets child know what you like Increases self-esteem Adds to warmth of the relationship Makes both parent and child feel good!	Terrific counting! I like the way you're playing so quietly. You have wonderful ideas for this game. I'm proud of you for being polite. You did a nice job on that building. Your design is pretty. Thank you for showing the colors to me.

"Do" and "Don't" Skills for Special Playtime
Parent Handout *(continued)*

Rule	Reason	Examples
Ignore inappropriate behavior (unless dangerous or destructive) a. Don't look at child, speak, smile, frown, etc. b. Ignore every time c. Expect behavior to increase at first	Avoids increasing bad behavior Decreases some behaviors Helps child notice difference between your responses to good and bad behavior	**Child:** (Sasses parent, then picks up toy) **Parent:** (Ignores sass; praises picking up) **Child:** (hits parent) **Parent:** (GAME STOPS; can't be ignored)
Don't give *commands*.	Doesn't allow child to lead Can cause unpleasantness Child obedience will be taught later	*Indirect* Will you hand me that paper? Could you tell me the alphabet? *Direct* Look at this. Please tie your shoe. Come here.
Don't ask *questions*.	Leads the conversation instead of following Many are commands or require an answer May seem like you aren't listening or disagree with child	That's a blue one, right? What color is this? Are you having fun? You want to play with the wastebasket?
Don't *criticize*.	Doesn't work to decrease bad behaviors Often increases the criticized behavior May lower the child's self-esteem Creates an unpleasant interaction	You're being naughty. I don't like it when you talk back. Don't scribble on your paper. No, honey, that's not right. That design is ugly.

Suggested Toys for Special Playtime

Creative construction toys, like:

Building Blocks	Duplos®	Magnetic Blocks
Bristle Blocks®	Waffle Blocks®	Erector Set®
Magnetic Picture Board	Crayons and Paper	Chalkboard/Colored Chalk
Legos®	Tinker Toys®	Lincoln Logs®
Toy Garage with Cars	School Bus with Riders	Toy Farm with Animals
Dollhouse with People	Mr. Potato Head®	Constructo-Straws®

Toys to Avoid During Special Playtime

Toys that encourage rough play, like:
bats, balls, boxing gloves, punching bag.

Toys that lead to aggressive play, like:
toy guns, toy swords, toy cowboys and Indians, superhero figures.

Toys that could get out of hand and require limit-setting, like:
paints, scissors, clay.

Toys that have pre-set rules, like:
board games, card games.

Toys that discourage conversation, like:
books, audiotapes.

Toys that lead parent or child to pretend they are someone else, like:
puppets, costumes, toy phones, dolls.

Special Playtime Homework Sheet

Did you practice play therapy for five minutes?

DATE	YES	NO	Note Any Problems That Came Up
MONDAY			
TUESDAY			
WEDNESDAY			
THURSDAY			
FRIDAY			
SATURDAY			
SUNDAY			

DYADIC Parent Child Interaction Coding System (DPICS)
Clinically Modified Recording Form

Child's Name: _____   Date: _____

Parent's Name: _____

Observer's Name: _____

INTAKE: A B
TREATMENT SESSIONS: 1 2 3 4 5 6 7 8 9 10 11 12
BOOSTERS: A B C D

Parent Behaviors		Child Behaviors
Direct command followed by. . .		No opportunity
		Compliance
		Noncompliance
Indirect command followed by. . .		No opportunity
		Compliance
		Noncompliance
Descriptive statement		Disruptive behavior. . .
		Ignored
		Responded to
Reflective statement		Other child behavior
Unlabeled praise		Clinical Notes
Labeled praise		
Question		
Critical statement		
Other verbalization		

Summary of DPICS Code Definitions

Descriptive Statement: A declarative sentence or phrase that gives an account of the objects or people in the situation or the activity occurring during the interaction (e.g., You're building a pick-up truck; You're sitting quietly).

Reflective Statement: A declarative phrase or statement which immediately repeats the child's verbalization. The reflection may be exactly the same words the child said, may contain synonymous words, or may contain some elaboration upon the child's statement, but the basic content must be the same as the child's message (e.g., CHILD: I made a big square. PARENT: You made a big square inside this big circle.)

Unlabeled Praise: A nonspecific verbalization that expresses a favorable judgment on an activity, product, or attribute of the child (e.g., Great; Nice; Good work; Perfect!).

Labeled Praise: Any specific verbalization that expresses a favorable judgment upon an activity, product, or attribute of the child (e.g., That's a terrific house you made; You have a beautiful smile).

Question: A descriptive or reflective comment expressed in question form. Questions follow the child's activity rather than attempt to lead it (e.g., Do you want to play with the barn?). Some questions are differentiated from statements by voice inflection (e.g., That's the baby?).

Critical Statement: A verbalization that finds fault with the activities, products, or attributes of the child (e.g., You're being naughty; That's a sloppy picture).

Direct Command: A clearly-stated order, demand, or direction in declarative form. The statement must be sufficiently specific as to indicate the behavior that is expected from the child (e.g., Put your hands in your lap; Please put that block here).

Indirect Command: An order, demand, or direction for a behavioral response that is implied, nonspecific, or stated in question form (e.g., Put it here, OK?; Johnny!; Let's take out the red blocks).

Disruptive Behavior: Any *cry* (inarticulate utterance of distress), *yell* (loud screech, scream, shout, or loud crying, *whine* (words uttered in a slurring, nasal, high-pitched falsetto voice), *smart talk* (impudent or disrespectful speech such as, You're stupid; No!; I hate you; Why should I?; Oh, that's just great), *destructive* (destroys, damages, or attempts to damage any object such as throwing blocks at wall; banging Lincoln Log on table; kicking toy box), or *physical negative* (bodily attack or attempt to attack the parent, such as hitting; slapping; biting; pinching; throwing something at the parent; kicking; pulling hair; twisting finger; standing on toe).

Ignores: Parent remains silent, maintains a neutral facial expression, avoids or breaks eye contact with the child, and makes no movement in response to the child, except to turn away.

Responds To: Any verbal or nonverbal reaction by the parent following a disruptive child behavior.

No Opportunity: Child is not given an adequate chance to comply with a command (e.g., command is vague; behavior requested is not within the child's competence; parent quickly repeats a command; parent quickly issues another command; parent issues a command while child is already doing requested action; parent does the requested behavior for the child).

Compliance: Child obeys, begins to obey, or attempts to obey a direct or indirect parental command (e.g., PARENT: Draw a person. CHILD: [draws a face]).

Noncompliance: Child does not obey a direct or indirect parental command (e.g., ignoring parent; refusing to obey; counter-commanding; making an excuse; arguing).

Adapted and reprinted by permission from Eyberg, S.M. & Robinson, E.A. (1983). Dyadic Parent-Child Interaction Coding System: A manual. *Psychological Documents, 13,* Ms. No. 2582. (Available from Social and Behavior Sciences Documents, Select Press, P.O. Box 9838, San Rafael, CA 94912)

Staircase to Termination

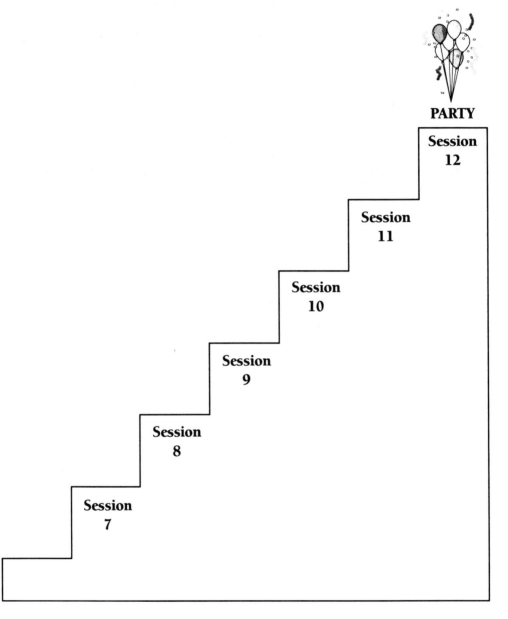

References

Achenbach, T. M. (1991). *Integrative Guide for the 1991 CBCL/4-18, YSR, and TRF Profiles.* Burlington: University of Vermont, Department of Psychiatry.

Achenbach, T. M. (1992). *Manual for the Child Behavior Checklist/2-3 and 1992 Profile.* Burlington: University of Vermont, Department of Psychiatry.

Axline, V. M. (1947). *Play Therapy.* Cambridge, MA: Houghton Mifflin Company, The Riverside Press.

Barkley, R. A. (1990). *Attention Deficit Hyperactivity Disorder.* New York: Guilford.

Berne, P. H., & L. M. Savary, L. M. (1990). *Building Self-Esteem in Children.* New York: Continuum Publishing Co.

Crary, E. (1993). *Without Spanking or Spoiling (Second Edition).* Seattle, WA: Parenting Press, Inc.

Dinkmeyer, D. & McKay, G. D. (1983). *Systematic Training for Effective Parenting of Teens.* Circle Pines, MN: American Guidance Service.

Eyberg, S. M. (1992). Parent and teacher behavior inventories for the assessment of conduct problem behaviors in children. In L. VandeCreek, S. Knapp, & T. Jackson (Eds.), *Innovations in Clinical Practice: A Sourcebook,Volume II.* Sarasota, FL: Professional Resource Press.

Eyberg, S. (1988). Parent-Child Interaction Therapy: Integration of traditional and behavioral concerns. *Child and Family Behavior Therapy,* 10, 33-46.

Eyberg, S. M. & Boggs, S. R. (1989). Parent training for oppositional-defiant preschoolers. In C. E. Schaefer & J. M. Briesmeister (Eds.), *Handbook of Parent Training: Parents as Co-Therapists for Children's Behavior Problems.* New York: John Wiley & Sons.

Freeman, T. (1982). *It's My Body.* Seattle, WA: Parenting Press.

Gardner, R. A. (1973). The Talking, Feeling, and Doing Game. Cresskill, NJ: Creative Therapeutics.

Gesme, C. (1987). Ups and Downs with Feelings Game. Minnetonka, MN.

Harter, S. & Pike, R. (1984). *The Pictorial Scale of Percieved Competence and Social Acceptance for Young Children.* Child Development, 55, 1969-1982.

Heegaard, M. (1991). *When Someone Very Special Dies.* Bursville, NC: Rainbow Connection.

Hembree-Kigin, T. L. & McNeil, C. B. (1995). *Parent-Child Interaction Therapy.* New York: Plenum Publishing Corporation.

Hughes, J. N. & Baker, D. B. (1990). *The Clinical Child Interview.* New York: Guilford.

Kanfer, R., Eyberg, S. M., & Krahn, G. L. (1992). Interviewing strategies in child assessment. In C. E. Walker & M. C. Roberts (Eds.), *Handbook of Clinical Child Psychology (Second Edition).* New York: John Wiley & Sons.

Kazdin, A. E. (1988). *Child Psychotherapy: Developing and Identifying Effective Treatments.* New York: Pergamon Press.

Knell, S. M. (1993). *Cognitive-Behavioral Play Therapy.* Northvale, NJ: Jason Aronson, Inc.

Kovacs, M. (1985). *The Children's Depression Inventory.* Psychopharmacology Bulletin, 21, 995-998.

Kovacs, M. (1992). *Children's Depression Inventory Manual.* North Tonawanda, NY: Multi-Health Systems.

Levy, R. (1995). Short-term therapy with the AD/HD and Oppositional Child. Workshop presented at the Institute for Professional Training in Brief Therapy, Monterey, CA.

Long, S. (1986). Guidelines for treating young children. In K. MacFarlane & J. Waterman (Eds.), *Sexual Abuse of Young Children.* New York: Guilford.

Lyman, R. & Hembree-Kigin, T. L. (1994). *Mental Health Interventions with Preschool Children.* New York: Plenum Publishing Corporation.

Mash, E. J., & Barkley, R. A. (1989). *Treatment of Childhood Disorders.* New York: Guilford.

McGinnis, E. & Goldstein, A. P. (1990a). *Skillstreaming in Early Childhood.* Champaign, IL: Research Press Company.

McGinnis, E. & Goldstein, A. P. (1990b). *Skillstreaming in Early Childhood: Program for Ms.* Champaign, IL: Research Press Company.

Nemiroff, M. A. & Annunziata, J. (1990). *A Child's First Book About Play Therapy.* Washington, DC: American Psychological Association.

O'Connor, K. J., & Schaefer, C. E. (1994). *Handbook of Play Therapy (Volume Two: Advances and Innovations).* New York: John Wiley & Sons.

Robin, A. (1976). The turtle technique: An extended case study of self-control in the classroom. *Psychology in the Schools,* 13, 449-453.

Schaefer, C. E., & O'Connor, K. J. (1983). *Handbook of Play Therapy.* New York: John Wiley & Sons.

Schroeder, C. S. & Gordon, B. N. (1991). *Assessment and Treatment of Childhood Problems.* New York: Guilford.

Shapiro, L. E. (1993). *The Book of Psychotherapeutic Games.* King of Prussia, PA: The Center for Applied Psychology, Inc.

Sloves, R., & Peterlin, K. B. (1993). Where in the world is. . . My father? A time-limited play therapy. In T. Kottman & C. Schaefer (Eds.), *Play Therapy in Action: A Casebook for Practitioners.* Northvale, NJ: Jason Aronson, Inc.

Spielberger, C. D. (1973). *Manual for the State-Trait Anxiety Inventory for Children.* Palo Alto, CA: Consulting Psychologists Press.

Walker, C. E., & Roberts, M. C. (1992). *Handbook of Clinical Child Psychology (Second Edition).* New York: John Wiley & Sons.

Index

About the Authors

Cheryl Bodiford McNeil, Ph.D. is a child clinical psychologist and Assistant Professor in the Department of Psychology at West Virginia University. Her clinical and research interests are in the areas of child behavior therapy, abuse and neglect, and school-based interventions for ADHD. She is the developer of the ADHD Classroom Kit: An Inclusive Approach to Behavior Management and the co-author of *Parent-Child Interaction Therapy*.

Toni Hembree-Kigin, Ph.D. is an independent practitioner and consultant in Tempe, Arizona, specializing in child clinical psychology and early intervention. Dr. Hembree-Kigin is the co-author of *Parent-Child Interaction Therapy* and *Mental Health Interventions with Preschool Children*. Prior to beginning her early childhood mental health practice, Dr. Hembree-Kigin was on the faculty at the University of Alabama where she co-directed the Alabama Child and Family Research Clinic and trained doctoral students in the psychological assessment and treatment of children.

Sheila M. Eyberg, Ph.D. is a Professor in the Department of Clinical and Health Psychology at the University of Florida. Dr. Eyberg is the developer of Parent-Child Interaction Therapy (PCIT). PCIT is a behavioral family intervention for young conduct problem children that involves direct coaching of parent-child interactions. Among Dr. Eyberg's many accomplishments is an extensive research record in the area of child treatment and assessment. She currently is the principal investigator on a large-scale NIMH grant investigating the effectiveness of PCIT. Dr. Eyberg has served on many committees (e.g., American Psychological Association) and is a past-president of the Section on Clinical Child Psychology and the Society for Pediatric Psychology.